"I'm so excited for the world to have the ⟨...⟩ Clint's uniquely powerful story, not bec⟨...⟩ career in the NFL, but because he's a gu⟨...⟩ to life than football. His love for God shines through the pages of this book, and will minister to your heart."

MATTHEW WEST /
GRAMMY NOMINATED RECORDING ARTIST AND SONGWRITER

//

"I've known a good number of professional athletes who desire to honor Christ; Clint Gresham is one who has effectively used his NFL career as a gospel platform. *Becoming* is a courageous book, in which Clint deals with things everyone can relate to, inside or outside of sports. He has faced his fears and insecurities, and is transparent about them and his journey toward healing and wholeness. He speaks honestly and openly about things that nearly all professional athletes—and the rest of us too—have often felt, but rarely speak about, and almost never publicly. I admire Clint's honesty and courage, but most of all his trust in Jesus, the Audience of One who sees all and knows all, and accepts and transforms us by His redemptive grace. Clint appeals to the timeless wisdom of God's Word, making this much more than a book of personal opinions. I was genuinely touched by *Becoming*, and I think you will be too."

RANDY ALCORN /
AUTHOR OF *Heaven, The Treasure Principle,* AND *Courageous*

"*Becoming* is a journey with the author, Clint Gresham, through his life's processes as a believer in Jesus and an NFL player. In the ecstasy of our greatest heights and the pain and powerlessness of our deepest valleys, Clint reminds us that the real tests come in the form of true identity, courage, vulnerability, and love. I recommend you read this book and allow God to highlight your own place in the journey to *Becoming* a whole and healthy person."

DANNY SILK /
FOUNDER AND PRESIDENT OF LOVING ON PURPOSE
AND LOP LIFE ACADEMY, AND AUTHOR OF
Keep Your Love On AND *Culture of Honor*

//

"I don't understand what it feels like to be a professional athlete or to compete in the Super Bowl but I do intimately understand the struggles of fear, rejection, and insecurity. This is why *Becoming* is such an important book. It's a book that speaks to everyone— and I mean *everyone*. Through blunt and vulnerable honesty, Clint Gresham invites us into his story but more importantly, invites us into the story of God and to find our true identity in Christ."

REV. EUGENE CHO /
PASTOR AND HUMANITARIAN
AUTHOR OF *Overrated: Are We More in Love With the Idea
of Changing the World Than Actually Changing the World?*

//

"*Becoming* will challenge you and inspire you to become the person God has created you to be!"

DERWIN L. GRAY /
LEAD PASTOR TRANSFORMATION CHURCH
AUTHOR OF *Limitless Life: You Are More Than Your Past
When God Holds Your Future*

"My friend Clint Gresham is a man who fears and loves the Lord. In his new book *Becoming*, he encourages the reader to 'embrace the process.' We all experience setbacks and disappointments; this book will challenge you to find the joy of the Lord in all seasons.

JOHN BEVERE /
AUTHOR/MINISTER, MESSENGER INTERNATIONAL

//

"Clint and I have become close friends over the years. We've celebrated each other's victories together as well as walked through some of life's most painful situations. Through it all, Clint has shown what it is to keep his heart anchored in the truth that unconditional love and acceptance are only found in Christ. In *Becoming*, Clint shares this journey of finding true identity and gives invaluable keys on how to live full of the confidence available to us as believers. I am thankful for his vulnerability that challenges us to consider our motivations and how we define success. This book exposes the lies that keep us from fulfilling our purpose and shows us how to walk in the freedom of knowing that through Christ we are capable of anything. Clint's insight into the heart of the Father is freeing, showing us that true success is found in becoming who God has created us to be. This book is life changing and sure to inspire and impart freedom to many!

CHRIS QUILALA /
SINGER-SONGWRITER FOR JESUS CULTURE

//

"*Becoming* puts the emphasis right where it needs to be—on the grace-filled process God offers to all who choose to be fearless and vulnerable enough to become 'smooth stones' in the hand of God."

GREGG JOHNSON /
FOUNDER OF J12

"I have been a fan of Clint's for some time, not because I know anything about long snapping but because of his authenticity, humility, love for others, and love for the Lord. His honest reflection of his time spent in the NFL, and his struggle with the departure from it is an incredible read that will be sure encourage and lead you in your own journey."

CRAIG GROSS /
FOUNDER OF XXXCHURCH.COM

//

"I hear from people daily who are trying to outrun difficult life circumstances and the emotional pain that follows. In *Becoming* Clint gives us a powerful truth laced with permission and grace to come out of hiding, embrace our pain, and author the next beautiful chapter of our lives. This book is packed with important, relevant, and timely wisdom."

MILES ADCOX /
OWNER/CEO OF ONSITE AND SPEAKER

//

"I wish I had read *Becoming* when I was a kid beginning my athletic pursuits. Learning who we are, what makes us of worth, and why we don't need to perform in sports and life are just a few of the important lessons Clint shares. Even today, even though I've personally learned many of the same lessons Clint discusses, I found myself drawn to each chapter as a refreshing reminder of how we should live."

RYAN HALL /
TWO-TIME OLYMPIAN, AMERICAN RECORD
HOLDER IN THE HALF MARATHON, AND THE FASTEST
AMERICAN TO EVER RUN THE MARATHON

"Clint Gresham's book *Becoming* is an amazing message of courage and hope. His experience in the NFL has helped him realize the challenges of having a healthy identity. So often we let the world around us define who we are. You are more than what you do. You are more then a job. Clint is practical and powerful as he gives insights to help you become the person you have always wanted to be."

CASEY TREAT /
SENIOR PASTOR OF CHRISTIAN FAITH CENTER

///

"Super Bowl-winning professional athlete Clint Gresham recognizes the dangers of replacing who we are with what we do, what we have, or what we want. Through this discovery process, Clint has created a playbook of his own, one that allows us, the readers, to remain focused on growing to be the unique person our heavenly Father created us to. become."

BIL CORNELIUS /
BEST-SELLING AUTHOR AND PASTOR OF CHURCH UNLIMITED

///

"What a courageous book! Clint holds no punches in sharing out of a place of vulnerability. In his journey out of fear, rejection, loss, and pain we, the readers, can see a picture of our own overcoming journeys. You can tell that Clint's identity and own coach-ability have created a masterful coaching resource to help you make the types of choices that will lead you into your real identity. I love how Clint has taken his platform and turned it into a place from which he can speak as sometimes a mentor, sometimes a teacher, sometimes a father, and always a friend.

SHAWN BOLZ /
TV PERSONALITY AND AUTHOR OF *Translating God*

CLINT GRESHAM

Becoming
First Edition Trade Book, 2017

Copyright © 2017 by Clint Gresham

Scripture quotations are identified as follows:

Scriptures marked ESV are from the ESV® Bible (The Holy Bible, English Standard Version®), copyright © 2001 by Crossway, a publishing ministry of Good News Publishers. Used by permission. All rights reserved.

Scriptures marked ISV are taken from Scripture taken from the Holy Bible: International Standard Version®. Copyright © 1996-forever by The ISV Foundation. ALL RIGHTS RESERVED INTERNATIONALLY. Used by permission.

Scriptures marked NKJV are taken from the New King James Version®. Copyright © 1982 by Thomas Nelson. Used by permission. All rights reserved.

Scriptures marked NLT are taken from the Holy Bible, New Living Translation, copyright ©1996, 2004, 2007, 2013, 2015 by Tyndale House Foundation. Used by permission of Tyndale House Publishers, Inc., Carol Stream, Illinois 60188. All rights reserved.

Scriptures marked The Message are taken from THE MESSAGE, copyright © 1993, 1994, 1995, 1996, 2000, 2001, 2002 by Eugene H. Peterson. Used by permission of NavPress. All rights reserved. Represented by Tyndale House Publishers, Inc.

Scripture quotations marked (NIV) are taken from the Holy Bible, New International Version®, NIV®. Copyright © 1973, 1978, 1984, 2011 by Biblica, Inc.™ Used by permission of Zondervan. All rights reserved worldwide. www.zondervan.com The "NIV" and "New International Version" are trademarks registered in the United States Patent and Trademark Office by Biblica, Inc.™

To order additional books:
www.amazon.com
www.clintgresham.com

E-book also available

ISBN: 9780-9988578-1-7

Inspira Literary Solutions, Gig Harbor, WA
Book Design: Ashton Owens, Wheelhouse Creative
Printed in the USA by Pritopya

To Phil

You were always available . . .
and I'm forever marked because of it.
I miss you.

becoming

verb be·com·ing \-ˈkə-miŋ\
come to a place, come (to be or do something)

adjective be·com·ing \-ˈkə- miŋ\
having a pleasing or attractive effect or appearance

Dear friends, we are already God's children,
but he has not yet shown us what we will be like when
Christ appears. But we do know that we will be like
him, for we will see him as he really is.

1 John 3:2

Now we see things imperfectly, like puzzling reflections
in a mirror, but then we will see everything with perfect
clarity. All that I know now is partial and incomplete,
but then I will know everything completely,
just as God now knows me completely.

1 Corinthians 13:12

CONTENTS

I once heard someone say that life is nothing more than a series of setbacks, and our happiness is determined by how we respond to them. Although I hate that statement because of its pessimistic focus, I can't help but accept its truth. The pressures, expectations, heartaches, and disappointments this side of Heaven are unbiased. Each one of us will experience them.

When I played for the Seattle Seahawks, I used to drive into downtown Seattle to Pioneer Square and hand out cheeseburgers, which I had crammed into my team-issued backpack, to homeless people. As much as it was for them, it was also for me. It helped me stay close to the reality that there were much greater issues in life than whether or not I played well, our team won or lost a Super Bowl, or my life stayed comfortable. It helped me to see that my life wasn't all that different from those people. That with just a few bad breaks or poor decisions, maybe I could be there, too . . . waiting for someone to bring me a hot meal on a dark, cold, and wet Seattle night.

When Jesus said, "Don't worry about tomorrow," I think He meant more than just, "Don't get stressed out." I think He also meant that to put too much focus on something in the future, or a particular outcome, ultimately robs us of the joy of the present moment. It seems to me this is the key to putting us back together, where there was once brokenness. To put off our joy until we don't feel down about something may result in never feeling joy at all. And to never let ourselves feel sad may result in never experiencing the euphoria of standing in the comforting presence of a loving, heavenly Father, who wants very much to be known by us.

All of us are in process. All of us have had setbacks. What causes joy to grow and fear to run is making the conscious choice to accept that the good times in life are God loving us, and the tough times in life are God growing us. We need them both. I'm realizing more and more that unchecked pain and disappointment may be the beginning of the breach in the paper thin barrier between my world and the world of my friends I gave food to.

Life is a gift, and while I hate to acknowledge how brutal it can be, I'm learning to hold heartbreaks a little bit closer. I'm not saying we should make our identity our pain; that only makes us victims. I am suggesting we actually let ourselves experience our pain enough to allow it to be filtered through who God says we are, so we can learn and grow from it.

So let's keep showing up. You win if you don't quit. Here's to loving the process on the journey to wholeness.

Gresh
Dallas, Texas
May, 2017

WHOLE/NESS:

"GIVING UP HOPE FOR A BETTER PAST, RELINQUISHING CONTROL FOR A PERFECT FUTURE, AND CHOOSING JOY AND COURAGE RIGHT WHERE OUR FEET ARE."

CLINT GRESHAM

WHO DO YOU THINK YOU ARE?

Being on an NFL team is like trying to hold on to a speeding train. You're either getting thrown off, trying to hold on to the spot you have, or trying to get back on the train. But no one ever looks back. Once the train is gone, you're better off trying to find another way home because no one on the train is waiting for you. They're all too busy holding on as tightly as you tried to.

SUPER BOWL XLIX

Any football player who has participated in a Super Bowl knows how stressful it is. While players may say in interviews and press conferences how much they loved it, in the safety of their closest confidants, they will likely tell you nothing compares to the pressure of that week.

For the Seahawks, the week leading up to the 2015 game against the Patriots seemed to bleed the entire training room of Pepto Bismol as we all battled what were delicately called "nervous bowel movements." Who knew the game America loves so much could have such a profound stress effect on the human body? Some turned to drugs and alcohol. Some turned to women. Some would gag themselves till they threw up. All in an attempt to manage the intensity of the world they found themselves in.

I didn't see the infamous interception thrown on the one-yard line to assure the win for the New England Patriots in Super Bowl 49. I was too busy trying to make sure I didn't screw up the snap for the PAT (point after touchdown). When I realized what happened, I literally fell to the ground. As the Patriots stormed the field, I found myself, along with the 114 million people watching, in utter disbelief.

The locker room wasn't much better. Some guys were crying, some were cursing, and some were screaming; one guy was yelling about not getting the ball handed off to him. To say it was tense is a gross understatement. Coach Carroll looked at me after offering a few lifeless words to the team and said, "Gresh, talk to us." That had been my cue over the previous three years to pray for our team. We all took a knee, and I mustered up the best prayer I could come up with. I thanked God for the opportunity and prayed He would use this experience for our good. It felt hollow even to me. My soul was tormented by the trauma of the moment. This storm shook many of us to the very core of who we were—or who we thought we were.

WHO IS THE REAL YOU?

What do you say when someone asks you about yourself—the typical party scenario where everyone is standing around making small talk? When that happens, most of us go straight to the one thing that gives us the greatest sense of accomplishment—the thing we are most proud of. You might call it our default identity. Things like,

"I'm a musician."

"I'm the president of a bank."

"I'm in graduate school."

Sometimes you can really wow people with your default identity, something like, "I play professional football." And, oh yeah, "I won a Super Bowl."

That's exactly how I *don't* lead off a conversation. Yes, I did win a Super Bowl—and played in a second one— and it was cool, really cool! But honestly, the thing that could be my greatest sense of identity (these days, anyway) is way lower on my priority scale than you might think. What I'm more likely to say when asked that question are things like, "I'm a husband. I'm a friend. I'm a Jesus guy. I'm a mentor to some really amazing young adults who are going to change the world some day."

Sure, it's tempting to play the professional football card. It's an easy way to get validation, acceptance, and even love of sorts. It's like a cheap drug. And, historically, I've liked that cheap drug.

WANTING TO MATTER

Football was my identity all through middle school, high school, and well into college. My dad played football at the University of Texas back in the 70s. Add that I grew up in Texas and it was assured I was groomed to love the game.

I can remember going to Darrel K. Royal stadium as a kid and looking at 80,000 people cheering on the players. These men were gods—worshipped by the masses! What is it about sports that brings that out in people? It doesn't seem to matter if it's a Super Bowl or a kids' lacrosse game. Sports pull us into real-time dramas and competitiveness and give us a temporary escape from our world. It's a win-win situation for all involved—relief for fans and affirmation for the athletes.

I'll never forget being 11 years old and going to a UT football camp with my friend Walker. He and I were on the 10th floor of the dorm when we looked down the hallway and saw our favorite Longhorn football player. We were shocked and awestruck. He was our idol! We raced down the hallway and must've freaked him out because he quickly hopped into the elevator and punched the button to close the doors.

Not allowing defeat, we raced down ten flights of stairs, jumping from platform to platform, trying to make it down to the lobby in time to see him again. We actually beat him! When the elevator door opened and we saw him standing there, I swear we heard the sound of trumpets and angels singing hallelu-jah. We didn't say a word to him, but I'll still never forget the goose bumps on my arms just from being in his presence. It was nearly two decades ago, but I still remember it. I idolized that man. But why? I didn't know anything about his character or the type of person he was. All I knew was that he was good at playing football.

I was moved up to the varsity football team as a sophomore in high school even after sitting out the previous two seasons due to injuries. In high school in South Texas, getting moved up to varsity as a sophomore was the equivalent of being a Super Bowl MVP. It was quite honestly the biggest status symbol around at the time.

I didn't get my letterman's jacket until the following April, and by that time in Corpus Christi it was hot and humid, but I didn't care. You'd better believe that the amount of sweat pouring out of me and the risk of heatstroke was nothing in compar-ison to the flood of endorphins that raced through my brain when someone noticed me (a 16-year-old sophomore) wearing a letterman's jacket.

Soon, I realized the harder I worked the better I got at foot-ball. And, when I was better at football, I got more atten-tion from others. Being good at football made me matter. I noticed that people seemed to esteem me more when I was wearing my letterman's jacket or after I'd just helped win a game. It was an addiction just like any other addiction, except the chemicals were coming from my body instead of from something external. I placed my value, my worth, and my identity in being just like the "gods" I watched at Darrel K. Royal stadium as a boy. It was so simple and so insidious. You see, I started to believe validation comes from doing and acceptance comes from performing. *If you aren't striving, you aren't worthy of love.* This is what I told myself—and it was the biggest trap I've ever fallen into.

Sports are great and valuable, but they are terrible fathers. Sports will give you identity and affirmation just like a father should, but they make you perform for it. If you aren't performing well, you can't count on them to come through for you in your search for meaning. The same is true for anything else in which we might put our identity.

Why do you think so many child actors, former pro athletes, or former musicians are an absolute mess when they finish their time of notoriety? It's because when you throw everything you are into a single pursuit and come to the end, it's crushing (you didn't just lose your job; you lost you). When you get what you worked for and it's not what you thought it would be, it's equally crushing.

Rarely have I met someone at the top of his or her industry who is not only incredible at his or her career but is also an incredible spouse or parent. Not because it isn't possible, but because to reach that level, things must be sacrificed. In the hunt for greater accomplishment, not only are we building our

" WHEN YOUR

IDENTITY

IS IN WHAT YOU DO,
THEN YOUR MOST BASIC LIFE

FOUNDATION

IS BEING BUILT UPON SOMETHING

SHAKABLE. "

#BECOMINGBOOK

life upon things that can be taken away, but in the meantime, the ones closest to us can often get our paltry leftovers. Everyone loses.

When your identity is in what you do, then your most basic life foundation is being built upon something shakable. And there is nothing more terrifying than finding out you've built your life—every waking moment—on something that can be taken away in an instant.

Every single one of us wants to matter—to be relevant and accepted and loved. However, not very many people are willing to admit that the way they are trying to meet this basic need will simply leave them wanting more.

TRYING ALL THE THINGS THAT DON'T WORK

I pretty much tried it all to be okay with who I was—sports, performance, girls, drugs, alcohol, and even pornography. The amazing (amazingly sad) thing about these things is that they all provide a temporary sense of relief, power, or validation. The problem is this: each time you turn to them, the amount of time that passes until you need them again decreases. And, generally, the amount you need to get the same effect constantly increases. It's the reason God is so serious about wanting us to place our identity in Him, not them. He wants to be number one in our lives. Is He an egotist? Not at all! The reason God hates all these things is because He hates seeing us waste our lives, not because He wants to spoil our "fun." He wants us to trust Him and know that all these things will only lead to more darkness, isolation, and shame. He knows He is the only One who can truly satisfy the longing of the human soul.

In the world of professional sports, I see this striving for worth constantly. There is nothing that concerns me more than when I see someone start his sports career being humble and re-latable and then slowly morph into an unfamiliar creature that *must* have the drug of affirmation. It becomes obvious that these athletes aren't rooted in their original design—the unique way God has created them. In fact, they have no roots at all and find their significance in others stroking their ego. And when the "identity" of being a professional athlete is stripped away (and it will be), what will they have left?

The statistics for ex-NFL athletes are staggering. Many are broke, divorced, or strung out on substances within just a few years. It's a predictable cycle. Let me explain it this way: You come from nothing (or at least not very much) and have played football your whole life to make things better for your-self and your family. It begins as an admirable journey. You have always been the best athlete everywhere you've ever been (which means you went through the same addiction cy-cle I went through for at least a decade). The neural pathways you've reinforced in your brain, which cause you to think and act a certain way, now look like the Grand Canyon. You re-ceive fame, millions of dollars, affirmation from women, and the obsession of fans—as long as you play well.

But what happens when football is gone? One hundred percent of NFL players will be former players at some point. If you have been addicted to the praise of man and have learned to rely on it through your football performance as your default identity, then when it's gone . . . you're gone.

I saw this in a men's group I was in with about ten other professional football players. As we were sitting around talking, a guy I had known for years began to cry. When he pulled himself together, he explained to us how anxious he was about getting cut because he was convinced he wasn't good at anything else. He was afraid he would be unemployed, out of money, and alone. My heart broke for him. It reminded me of the scene in the movie *Friday Night Lights*, when Boobie Miles wept in the car after finding out his football career was done. The idol he was chasing so hard (football) was slipping through his fingers, and he felt helpless and frantic as he tried to hold on to it.

FINDING OUT WHO I REALLY AM

Here's the bottom line: identity has nothing to do with what you do. It doesn't matter if you're a musician or CEO, a mother or father, a boyfriend or girlfriend, a four-star general, or even a Super Bowl-winning football player. Identity is who you are. It's not something you work for—it's something you work from. It isn't created, it's found. And, once you do, it's something you have to hold on to and never lose sight of.

While growing up, I had a close friend who was a good example of a person who had no sense of his own identity. When we got into high school, he started hanging out with a crowd of cowboy dudes for about a year or so. He started wearing Wranglers and big ol' belt buckles and boots to school. He even started chewing tobacco! I wasn't really into this scene, so we grew apart.

During my sophomore year, my friends and I started a punk band and were having tons of fun going to concerts and playing music. Before I knew it, my ol' buddy Scott (not his real name) ended up hanging out with us a lot and we became close again. He quit wearing cowboy stuff and started wearing band T-shirts, skater shoes, and Dickies shorts. It was weird, but we were glad he was hanging with us.

But then junior year rolled around, and Scott morphed into yet another phase. Suddenly he was into the hippie scene and starting going to reggae music festivals. He would wear moccasins and tie-dyed clothing to school. Now we were confused. Who was this guy? I certainly didn't know, and I don't think he did either.

Now, looking back, I realize what was going on. Scott had no sense of identity and no confidence in the unique things that made him Scott. My sincere hope for him would be that he has since discovered who he really is and will not continue wearing mask after mask to try and be relevant, noticed, and accepted. The good news I hope Scott has learned is that, when you know you are noticed and accepted by your Creator, being "relevant" and striving to fit in simply don't matter anymore.

This confusion and doubt—always trying to be someone else—is a problem as old as humanity itself. The first person to buy into this lie was Eve way back in the Garden of Eden. The devil told her if she ate the forbidden fruit, she would be like God. Satan asked Eve to perform for her identity. But what she failed to realize was she had already been made in the image of God. And, failing to trust the truth of who God made her to be, she reached out and took the temptation. She performed for her identity, and it only left her broken. (You can read this story for yourself in Genesis chapter 3.) It goes on to say that Eve handed the fruit to Adam who took a bite as well. That was when their eyes were opened. They saw they were naked and began to feel ashamed. They sewed fig leaves together to try and cover up their doubt, fear, and overwhelming sense of shame.

Here's how we can apply their story to our own lives: when we go rooting around in the trash can for counterfeit fathers—counterfeit voices—who promise us they will make us feel valued and loved, our situation only ends up more dire. And where do we end up? In doubt, fear, and shame just like they did.

GETTING OVER OUR SHAME

I'll never forget my freshman year homecoming dance. I was a 15-year-old BMOC (Big Man on Campus) and had finally rallied enough courage to ask out the girl I'd had a crush on since sixth grade. To say it was a terrifying experience is an understatement.

It was four o'clock and school had just let out. I dashed out of Mrs. Smith's class knowing my future homecoming date would be walking through the cafeteria where her mom would be picking her up. As I walked up to her, I trembled with fear. I had only one question to ask. With my voice cracking, I mustered, "Do you . . . want to go to homecoming with me?"

She smiled and said, "Yes!" After I picked myself up off the floor from shock, I quickly told her thank you, said I'd call her, and then sprinted out of the cafeteria. (I liken it to a bank robbery: you don't sit around or loiter after you got what you came for; you get out of there as quickly as possible!)

For dinner on the night of the dance, our group of friends went to Olive Garden (nothing but the best for my date). All the salad and breadsticks you could ever want? Sign me up. As we sat there through dinner, I kept grasping for things to talk about. I felt this nagging voice inside me telling me what a terrible date I was. *You're not a man. In fact, you'll never get married because you can't even take a girl out on a decent date to Olive Garden. Why are you so awkward? She probably isn't even having fun with you.*

I wish I could say I got this huge surge of confidence somewhere between my carb-loading on fettuccine alfredo and slurping down my 32-ounce Coke, but the night only got worse. When we finally got back to the school cafeteria for the pictures and dance, I had reached an all-time low. This was the point in my life I realized that when I'm nervous, I sweat. I sweat, like, a lot. Anyone who went to high school with me would know this. (In fact, I come from a long line of sweaters. My father was a sweater, and I'm sure his father was a sweater as well.) So as we walked into the cafeteria, I was already soaked with sweat—so much that it was running down my face and soaking my sport coat.

As we were walking up to take pictures, one of my friends came up to me and threw open my jacket, pointed, and laughed— making a huge deal of what I was already so ashamed of (in front of my date, nonetheless). It was one of the most humiliating moments of my life. I was ashamed and embarrassed and disgusted with myself. I ran into the bathroom and did the only thing I could think of . . . I proceeded to put water in my mouth and made vomiting noises. Perfect excuse. I told my friends to tell my date I was sick and immediately called my dad to come pick me up. What a coward.

That humiliation stayed with me for years. I would be riding my bike to morning workouts my freshman year of college and would have a flashback to that night, which would lead to an assault of the most demeaning self talk you can imagine. I was so embarrassed I couldn't even face that girl again. If I saw her walking down the hallway at school, I would walk the other direction. It's amazing what shame will do to us.

Why did this event have so much power over me? I realize now, in retrospect, that school dances (and other similar occasions) were awkward for me mostly because my worth was based on whether someone liked me. That always led to performance, which then created anxiety because I had so much to lose. The truth was, I had no idea who I was. A football player? A student? A son? A terrible date? I had no clue. Looking back, I can see I was a desperate, lonely, and anxious teenager looking for anything and anyone to reassure me that I was cool and that I was worthy of love.

IDENTITY RELEASED

During those years when I was striving so hard to find my identity, I worried (needlessly, I later found out) that people's love and acceptance for me—my parents included—were based on how well I performed. I desperately needed affirmation. As people looked into my eyes, I wondered if they could hear my preoccupied mind asking: *Am I okay? Am I good enough? I will do anything you want if you can just tell me that. Help me feel okay. Tell me good things about me because all I hear in my own head is all the ways I'm not measuring up.* So exhausting!

For years, I didn't know or understand who God had created me to be as His son. I looked at my heavenly Father through the same lens through which I looked at football, my counterfeit father. Perform, and you will be accepted. I genuinely loved God with everything that was in me. But, because I

"I BELIEVE YOU WERE CREATED TO ACCOMPLISH GREAT THINGS."

didn't have a revelation of God's love for me, I offered other people the same formula: Be good and you are good. Perform well and you'll be loved. I desperately wanted them to know God but, because I didn't understand my own identity, I couldn't offer them anything more than my own hamster wheel of performance.

There came a time my two brothers, my dad, and I were together at one brother's fraternity skeet shoot. In an act of spontaneous affection, Dad pulled all three of us together with his arms around us and prayed for us, speaking out loud a father's blessing. It was a moment I never knew I needed, but it was like water to my thirsty soul. I had always known my dad loved me and was proud of me. Those things were never in question. What I didn't know was that moment would solidify something in me for the rest of my life; no matter where I went, he was for me. There was nothing I could do in life in which he would be disappointed. Whatever my desire was, he was supporting me. To a kid who thought his identity was football or nothing, this was a huge gift. My father released identity in me that day.

Identity doesn't necessarily have to be released, or "called out," by our parents (although it's sure great when it is). It can be called out by just about anyone like relatives, friends, coaches, teachers, pastors, or mentors. It's as simple as walking beside someone and saying: "I believe you were created to accomplish great things. You are created in the image of God. You are His beloved child and He is pleased in you. You have been uniquely blessed with special talents and callings." Calling out and releasing their identity is one of the greatest gifts we can give other people. You will be amazed at how people will come alive when they know someone is in their corner.

One of my favorite stories in the Bible is in the book of Matthew when Jesus was baptized by John.[1] John was out in the wilderness eating nothing but honey and locusts. (He certainly wasn't in ministry for the money; am I right?). When John saw Jesus, He told Him, "You're coming to me to be baptized? I need to be baptized by you!"

Jesus basically responded with, "Yeah, I get that, but this is how it needs to go." John ended up baptizing Him and the account goes on to say that the heavens were opened, the Spirit of God descended on Him, and the voice of the Father said audibly, "This is my beloved Son, in whom I am well pleased."

What is amazing to me was that this was *before* Jesus ever did any type of earthly ministry! The Father needed Jesus to work *from* His identity as God's Son, and not work *for* His identity. What that tells me is that the number one thing I need in my life to guard me from slipping back onto the hamster wheel of performance is a daily reminder of who God says I am. I need to hear from God daily, "Clint, you are my beloved son, in whom I am well pleased." We all need this reminder of who we are. We need to know that our value is secure and we are worthy of love.

_____

1   *Matthew 3:13-17*

Today God is saying to you, "You are my beloved child and I'm pleased in you." Meditate on that because it's true, and it's available to you for the asking. Then think about who you can pass along this same gift to: a friend? A sibling? Someone you mentor? We all have a responsibility not just to operate in our own God-given identity, but to release identity in other people. We have the power to affirm who they are and help them grow into what they were created to be.

PRETENDING: ANOTHER WAY TO FIND IDENTITY

I recently spoke at a men's conference in Pasco, Washington with my buddy Tyler Lockett. It was awesome to see him, and I was thankful to get one last road trip with a former Seahawks teammate. It was a powerful weekend of seeing over 1,100 men coming together to worship God and learn how to be better men.

The night before I spoke, our host took us out to a great seafood restaurant. As we sat down, a friendly waitress named Megan greeted us. She enthusiastically asked us in her fun British accent what we would like to drink. As I sat there and listened to her talk, I was taken aback by her accent. Running into a thick British accent in Eastern Washington is a rare event! When she came back with our drinks, I asked her, "That's such a cool accent; where are you from?"

In a perfectly clear American accent, she responded, "Oh, I'm from Everett, Washington—just north of Seattle." I was shocked.

She went on, "When it's late, it gets harder for me to talk." I didn't know what to think. As we continued our dinner, I would notice her going back and forth between an American accent and her *Downton Abbey* imitation. Finally I looked at Tyler and asked incredulously, "Is she faking this accent?!" We started laughing in complete confusion as to why this woman felt the need to talk in a way that was obviously unnatural to her.

When I got back to my hotel later that night, I had a realization. How often do I go into a room of people and do the exact same thing? Maybe it's not faking an accent. Maybe it's just trying to be funny. Trying to be relevant. Trying to be liked. We all have this deep desire in us to be accepted—naturally, we desire community. One of the most profound verses I have read in the Bible is, "A man who isolates himself seeks his own desire; he rages against all wise judgment."[2] That's because isolation goes against our original design. We were designed for belonging.

I began to have compassion for this woman. She was a chameleon . . . just like I can be sometimes, or my friend Scott, back in high school. Her struggle was just more obvious and outward than mine. I felt convicted, as I had laughed at her, not realizing her lack of authenticity was a part of the same disease that had afflicted me—the same one that has afflicted all of us.

Now, when I see those people like Megan who are so desperate for love, I hope I can meet them with the same grace God

---

2   *Proverbs 18:1, NKJV*

afforded me. That's obviously the kind of grace the apostle Paul found, too:

> . . . *We rely on what Christ Jesus has done for us. We put no confidence in human effort, though I could have confidence in my own effort if anyone could. Indeed, if others have reason for confidence in their own efforts, I have even more! . . . I once thought these things were valuable, but now I consider them worthless . . . Yes, everything else is worthless when compared with the infinite value of knowing Christ Jesus my Lord. For his sake I have discarded everything else, counting it all as garbage, so that I could gain Christ. (Philippians 3: 3-4, 7-9, NLT)*

I was desperate for love and Jesus found me to tell me who I am. He's after you, too.

DISCUSSION QUESTIONS

(001)
HOW DOES OUR IDENTITY
INFLUENCE THE LENS THROUGH
WHICH WE VIEW THE WORLD?

(002)
WHAT ROLE DO OTHER PEOPLE
HAVE IN SHAPING OUR IDENTITY?
WHO HAS HELPED SHAPE YOURS?

(003)
WHAT GIVES YOU THE GREATEST
SENSE OF ACCOMPLISHMENT IN
YOUR LIFE?

(004)
TO WHAT EXTENT DO YOU
PLACE YOUR IDENTITY IN YOUR
ACCOMPLISHMENTS? YOUR
RELATIONSHIPS?

"IDENTITY HAS NOTHING TO DO WITH WHAT YOU DO."

#BECOMINGBOOK

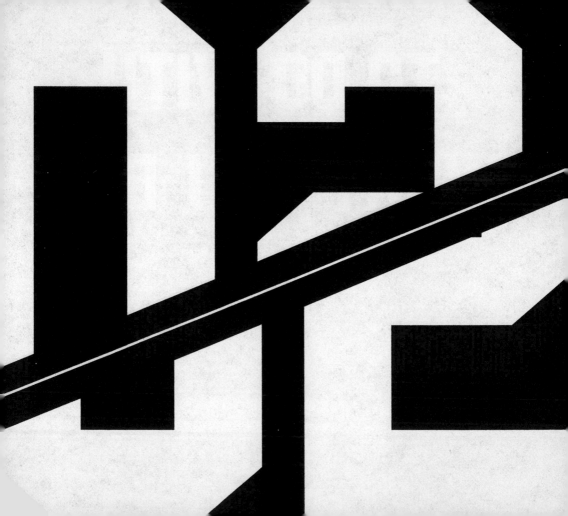

CAT'S IN THE CRADLE & THE MAN IN THE MOON

I don't know if there is a more damaging wound to the human soul than rejection. It's an insidious and diligent gremlin that burrows deep into our hearts, enmeshing itself with every part of our being. It doesn't just convince us we made a mistake; it proselytizes us to believe we *are* the mistake. In some ways, it seems to be woven into our DNA.

SEPARATED

All of us were born separated from God and painfully aware of our shortcomings. This is a by-product of the sin of our ancestors Adam and Eve. Where humans were designed to have a God nature, because of the decision of our first parents, we have a sin nature that separates us from a holy God.

I used to be frustrated with them—with Adam and Eve, I mean— because of that decision. I used to think that, when I got to Heaven, I would give them a piece of my mind! But it's not as if I've lived my life any better. The older and more experienced I get, the more I realize the Bible is right when it says, ". . . all have sinned and fall short of the glory of God."[3]

I was probably five years old in Sunday school when I first learned about the story of Adam and Eve. One of the symptoms of rejection is a victim mentality, which unconsciously looks for evidence that we are not worthy of love. As a child, I felt insecure and out of touch with whom God *actually* thought I was. When the Sunday school teacher began to teach about how God kicked His children out of the Garden of Eden, a little voice whispered a lie into my ear, "Make a mistake, and you're not welcome in this family. If you're not perfect, you aren't worthy of love. When you mess up, I don't want to even look at you." From that moment on, I carried a wound that took years to heal, a wound rooted in a lie I believed about God.

There are few things more effective than rejection in preventing us from becoming who God designed us to be. That's why it's such a huge scheme of the enemy to seed the lie of rejection into the human heart at a young age. The insidious thing about it is that, if you don't know something is a lie, you will forever live under its crushing weight, not knowing your predator is only a paper tiger.

What I seemed to have missed from my Sunday school teacher was that the reason God told Adam and Eve they couldn't stay in the Garden was that, if they were to eat of the Tree of Life

---

3   *Romans 3:23*

(which was the second tree in the garden), they would have been forever separated from God. God would have *never* been able to redeem them. It was more dangerous for them to live in the Garden in their fallen state than outside of the Garden. So, in His great love, God sent them out to make sure He could get them back. I wish I had learned this truth years earlier. It would have saved me a lot of effort—and a lot of woundedness.

The wounded soul will drive you to great lengths for comfort. It will cause you to sacrifice your morality and character through chemicals or promiscuity (or any number of other pursuits), all in the vain hope of one day feeling like you are worthy of love. With each scenario, the rejection tape will be re-played further driving a wedge between you and real relationships—isolating you and replicating itself in others through you.

THE CRY OF THE WOUNDED SOUL

My 14th birthday party, according to all in attendance, went down as one of the greatest nights in the history of Corpus Christi, possibly even since the creation of man. The night began like most eighth grade birthday parties, where we had a DJ and awkwardly danced close to girls we were too afraid to talk to in any other scenario. All I really remember is the DJ mostly played Korn and Limp Bizkit with the occasional Backstreet Boys, whom all the fellas loved to hate but secretly adored. I had invited about 50 people but had special plans over a long night with a select few.

As the final guest left around nine, five friends and I piled into the back of my stepdad's car to go to an old dive bar in Corpus to see the band Linkin Park. We didn't know anything about them at the time but were able to hang with them after their show and get autographs. Two weeks later, they were all over MTV.

After that, my stepdad drove us out to the beach where he had found a huge sand dune for us to play capture the flag in. He had gone out there earlier in the day and buried a giant light and a generator so the massive bowl we were in was practically illuminated from space. Just when I thought the night couldn't get any more fun, he took us to throw toilet paper in the trees of the houses of girls we went to school with. The night was about as perfect as I could have asked for.

What made the night so special for my friends and me was how my stepdad treated all of us. He was more like a big brother. He dismantled bombs for the Navy, drove a red sports car, took my friends and me to concerts, and participated in all kinds of pranks. My friends thought he hung the moon and, if you asked any of them today about him, they would say what a huge impact he had on all of us. He made me feel special, he made me cool to all my friends, and I felt so lucky to have him.

The birthday party happened a few weeks before my actual 14th birthday because the next day my stepdad was moving out. He was starting a job in another city but he and my mom were going to make it work long distance. Around 8:00 am the

"**WHOLENESS**

always seems to be a

| JOURNEY |

rather than a

DESTINATION."

next morning, I remember a knock on my door and him peeping his head in and saying goodbye. I didn't get out of bed. I really didn't understand the gravity of what was happening. I still regret groaning good-bye and rolling back over in my bed.

The last time I actually saw him was a year later in San Antonio, for a Blink 182 concert, just before my freshman year of high school. Things were different for some reason. I felt his distance but assumed it was because I was having so much fun with my friends and he wanted to give us space. He didn't even join in on the ice cube war we had down at the hotel pool after the concert, which surprised me.

During my sophomore year of high school, my mom told my brother and me that they were splitting up. We were crushed. We felt so abandoned. How could he do this to us? From that day on, something changed for both of us. Rejection reared its ugly head and convinced us we were unlovable. I tried calling my stepdad a few times later on to see how he was doing. But after years of only getting his answering machine, I finally gave up. Thoughts of shame and regret swarmed my mind, accusing me of all kinds of lies about what I had done wrong to make him not want to talk to me. It was one of the most painful periods of my life. I really don't remember much from that year.

I don't know if those kinds of wounds ever really go away. Though now I know I have been made whole, it seems those scars can retain a place in our heart. Wholeness always seems to be a journey rather than a destination. A process, not a product. One thing I've learned, though, is that, even though what my stepfather did was wrong, I had lifted him up to such a hero level in my own mind that I couldn't allow him to fail. I idolized him so much that I did exactly that: I turned him into an idol.

MODERN DAY IDOLATRY

You may be thinking, *Huh, an idol? Sounds like some weird archaic Bible word.* But an idol is nothing more than something external we use to satisfy an internal need that is meant to be satisfied by our Creator. That idol can be a person—like my stepdad was for me—or it can be a sport like football. But it can also be a boyfriend or girlfriend, having lots of money or a successful career you can be respected for, having the perfect-looking family, personal perfectionism, or self medication with drugs or alcohol. It can even be something noble and cherished like motherhood. It seems to be in our DNA to look to the external to satisfy us. I encourage you to be daring enough to ask yourself where you might be setting up these pseudo saviors to comfort your own wounded soul.

The Exodus story in the Bible perfectly illustrates this truth. An even bigger problem for Moses than getting the Israelites out of Egyptian slavery was freeing them from the thinking patterns of slavery. Even though they were free, they still behaved and thought like they were slaves. It was for this reason

YOU
NEED
HEROES

#BECOMINGBOOK

Moses had to be born in the palace of Pharaoh. God needed one person who knew how to act like royalty if He was going to train an entire nation in a new way of thinking!

One night Moses went up to the mountain to be with God. When he didn't come down when the people hoped, they all began to panic. They begged the next guy in line to make a calf (idol) out of gold for them to worship and give them the sense of security they craved. Considering all God had shown them, their faithlessness was a lot like a wife deciding to invite another man to her bed because her husband was late and she feared he'd never return. Not understanding how loved we are always drives us to do the ridiculous.

What led the Israelites to this point? They didn't trust. They didn't understand God's ways or what He wanted to do with them. They allowed insecurity and fear to cripple them to the point that an entire generation of their people didn't make it into the land God wanted to give them. In essence, they continued to go to bed with other gods to get their needs met. As God later pointed out, "For you have played the harlot against your God. You have made love for hire on every threshing floor." [4]

There are stories all over the Bible of these same types of events—of people looking to the created instead of the Creator for their security, comfort, and affirmation. The same problem rages on today with you and me. I didn't allow my stepdad to be human; I couldn't accept that he wasn't perfect.

---

4   *Hosea 9:1, NKJV*

It had to be my fault, right? The wound he inflicted into my eager heart cut deeper than it would have had my expectations not been so unreasonably high. But because they were so high, his failure crushed me.

Now, please hear me; I am all for people having heroes, looking up to someone, and seeking healthy validation. Our world needs it now, worse than ever! But when you make fallible human beings your idols and refuse to let them fail, you set yourself up as the sacrifice on the altar of your idolatry, leaving you with deep disillusionment and rejection.

I see this all the time in the church world. I think, because of social media, there has been a rise of the "celeb pastor" onto the scene, which didn't exist in previous decades. I don't believe social media caused it; I believe it was already in us to want to look perfect to everyone around us.

In the "church world," we lift up these men and women of God, who seem so perfect and holy, to the same level I did with my stepdad. In doing so, we don't let them fail. We hold them in the highest regard, forgetting they are oftentimes just as broken as we are. Their drive to build God's Kingdom can oftentimes be birthed as a reaction to pain intertwined with their calling from God. When we meet them and witness a first hand account of their humanity, we may find ourselves despising them because of the unrealistic expectation of faultlessness we put on imperfect people—people just like you and me . Yet again, we fall into the timeless trap of looking for something on the outside to satisfy us on the inside. We begin to base our identity not in who God says we are but on who an imperfect person says we are.

My wife experienced this phenomenon when she encountered a famous Christian speaker several years ago. Matti frequently listened to this teacher and aspired to be just like her. In Matti's eyes, she was practically the fourth member of the trinity.

I had the opportunity to speak at a few churches at which this woman had also spoken, and Matti happened to be with me on one of these occasions. While there, Matti mentioned to the pastors how much of an impression this woman had made on her. Independently, two separate women told Matti, "Let's send her a video encouraging her and telling her what an influence she has been in your life!" Both times, Matti felt uncomfortable with their suggestion, but went through with it begrudgingly. She was slightly embarrassed about the way these leaders chose to introduce her to her heroine.

Some time later, when Matti was out of town, she learned this woman was speaking at a local church. She was ecstatic. After an incredibly powerful word, Matti courageously went up to this woman to finally meet her hero face to face. Matti mentioned to her, "I'm the girl in the videos these women sent to you."

Matti's "hero" responded, "What are you, my stalker or something?" Matti was devastated.

I was disturbed at how careless this woman's words were. While I'm sure she was making a joke, those words were a crushing blow to my wife's spirit. People say, "Sticks and stones may break my bones but words will never hurt me." They seem to forget what Proverbs 18:21 says about how death and life are in the power of the tongue. I think a more appropriate children's rhyme would be, "Sticks and stones may break your bones but words can kill you."

How many people do you know who have been wounded like this when a leader—maybe a teacher or coach— glibly threw a barb into the heart of an admirer, leaving them scarred or embittered? Maybe this has even happened to you.

We open up our heart to people we look up to the most, not realizing they are just as broken as we are. They speak something carelessly or don't come through for us and, all of a sudden, we are left feeling absolutely rejected. As a way of coping with the pain of rejection, we end up turning to other idols because the original false gods don't come through for us. We can find ourselves entangled in all kinds of addictions and bondages because we didn't keep these people in the proper place. Idols beget more idols and our soul pain eventually needs stronger medicators.

No one is immune to experiencing the wound of rejection. The most hardened criminals in the world were once little boys and girls looking for someone they admired to affirm them. While they waited for love, a lie was planted in their heart,

"MY FATHER AND MOTHER MAY ABANDON ME, BUT THE LORD WILL TAKE CARE OF ME."

causing them to believe that the problem wasn't *what they did* but *who they were*. Each person who hasn't had their eyes opened to a loving, accepting God will continue to recreate the same pain or rejection in others. It's what the enemy of God has wanted to do since the Fall: try to cause people to feel just as depressed, rejected, and worthless as he is.

You need heroes, you need affirmation, you need people to speak into your life, and you need to remember that your heroes are humans who will fail you. Follow any person on the planet long enough and you will have enough sound bytes to make Hannibal Lector blush. Let people fail, invite God into your story, and allow Him to be the one who never fails you. Humanity can't carry the burden of perfection. "Becoming" whole will mean giving people the same grace you have been given. By making this conscious choice, you will be forever protected from the enemy's greatest trick: *rejection*.

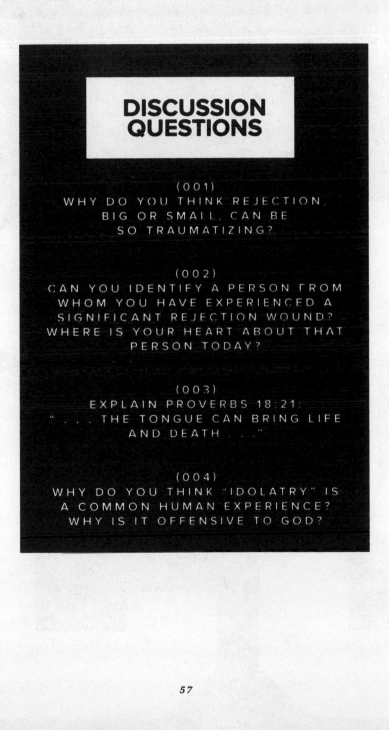

DISCUSSION QUESTIONS

(001)
WHY DO YOU THINK REJECTION,
BIG OR SMALL, CAN BE
SO TRAUMATIZING?

(002)
CAN YOU IDENTIFY A PERSON FROM
WHOM YOU HAVE EXPERIENCED A
SIGNIFICANT REJECTION WOUND?
WHERE IS YOUR HEART ABOUT THAT
PERSON TODAY?

(003)
EXPLAIN PROVERBS 18:21:
". . . THE TONGUE CAN BRING LIFE
AND DEATH . . ."

(004)
WHY DO YOU THINK "IDOLATRY" IS
A COMMON HUMAN EXPERIENCE?
WHY IS IT OFFENSIVE TO GOD?

03

JAIL-BREAK

After the Seattle Seahawks won the Super Bowl in 2014, we had our exit meeting the following Tuesday. I remember someone saying, "I keep waiting for it to sink in that we won the Super Bowl." I can't tell you how many times I heard that phrase. As time went on, I realized they weren't saying, "I keep waiting for it to happen," but, "I keep waiting for this thing I worked so hard for to satisfy me the way I hope it would." What they thought would give them contentment—the biggest sports victory imaginable—never did.

It was true for me, too. I thought winning a Super Bowl would complete me, that it would make me feel like a man and fill that empty feeling of inadequacy inside me that, if we're honest, every guy feels. But it didn't. Idols never fulfill what you hope they will.

LOOKING FOR LOVE IN ALL THE WRONG PLACES

Really, anything under the sun can be a false comfort for us. Just like the Israelites in the Bible, we look to tangible distractions as an escape from our pain. We feel rejection in our heart, so we look for something to help us feel worthy of love.

Girls put up their bikini pictures on Instagram to get more likes, we withhold love from people to get them to feel insecure and chase us, or we wear a letterman jacket in sweltering heat to get people to notice us. We employ all the tricks of the trade to find comfort in our fragile lives. Whether or not something is an idol for you is a matter of the heart.

God says everything we do unto Him He considers worship, which is defined as two simple things. First, it is to give something glory. All that means is to give something "weight." For example, you go to pick up your kid from school. You think all the kids there are wonderful but, to you, one of them is the "most wonderful": your kid! To hold something in high regard is to give it glory.

The second part of worship is to sacrifice something for it. An example of this is paying to see your favorite sports team play. You are forfeiting your resources because you want to see your favorite team. That is a sacrifice.

Do you like to play sports? By all means, do it as worship to God. Do you like to bake cookies? Do it as worship to God. Do you like to sing karaoke? Do it as worship to God. However, any activity absent of the presence of God has the potential to become idolatry. We are all worshipping something, and it's up to us to make sure our hearts are depending on the only thing that can truly hold us up—God and God alone.

It's when these things take the place of God as worship or we when turn to them for comfort in place of God that they become idols. For men, we have a tendency to look towards status, wealth, sexual conquest, or athletics as our idols. Women may also look to these kinds of things but also often turn to relationships, shopping, or body image for comfort. Below is a list of common idols that any of us may rely on for our identity, security, affirmation, or comfort:

01. PORNOGRAPHY

"My personal view is that, unfortunately,
availability of porn in some cases
has substituted for intimacy in personal
relationships, and that is unfortunate."
Scott Flanders, CEO of *Playboy*,
quoted in *CNN Money*, 2015

Porn may be one of the most dangerous drugs in our culture today. According to science, it has all the ramifications of an illicit drug with the most dangerous part being the deception that "it's not really hurting anyone if I look at it."

When I was in high school, porn was shameful. If someone knew you looked at porn, you were laughed at. The confusing thing was everyone I knew was looking at it. After volunteering with Young Life the past few years and being around high school kids of a different era, I am shocked at how, nowadays, it is not only accepted but celebrated.

Pornography creates a false image of what a woman should look like and is not based in reality. I have a friend named Craig who runs a ministry called XXX Church and he talks about how miserable women are in the sex industry. Drug use is rampant because these women are constantly trying to escape from the shame they feel from dehumanizing themselves for money. At the same time, many of them are being held against their will. I told some of the kids I work with about it and it totally changed their perspective. Suddenly, instead of objectifying the women, they felt remorse.

I completely understand the desire to look at pornography. There is nothing more alluring than the human body. If a bunch of guys are standing at the Grand Canyon and they see a naked woman, none of those guys are even going to notice the Grand Canyon. Pornography is also the perfect storm for addiction. Connect the beauty of the body God created, the secrecy of the Internet, and the very real need for intimacy and you have one of the most addictive things on the planet.

02. POSSESSIONS AND STATUS SYMBOLS

This idol is oftentimes socio-economically related. Someone who grows up having nothing sees people who have a lot and thinks that having a lot means having value. A person thinks, *This is what it means to be successful—drive this car, wear these clothes, be a part of this club, etc.* They live in an illusion where they are dominated by what others think of them; they thirst for significance.

When I was playing professional football, I knew a guy who was on the "practice squad." These are players who make significantly less than guys on the active roster and are often simply live hitting dummies. One day at practice, this guy pulled up in a Hummer and, the next very week, pulled up in a Mercedes—all while living in a month-to-month apartment. He couldn't really afford those cars. But, to him, they spelled success. For his entire life, he had watched what his heroes did and saw the money they spent trying to prove to the people around them they were powerful and worthy to be recognized.

I knew another teammate who would bring watches with him to each game. He had three or four and, between all of them, he had spent about $150,000. I asked him one time if the watches made him feel significant and he just laughed and said, "I've got an image to uphold, Gresh." I felt powerless to help this guy see how fragile his masculinity was. I mean, who was telling him he had to do that dance to continue receiving the applause he craved? Ultimately, anything you look to for significance, which can be taken away, is a horrible indicator of value.

Social status is the same way. Going after social status as a means of having value ultimately comes down to whom you reject, rather than whom you accept. It's twisted social segregation based on exclusivity where few are welcome and people are a means to an end. It means people are not inherently valuable and must conform to a certain mold to be worthy of love.

Growing up, I knew a guy who badly wanted to be a part of a certain fraternity group. He practically sold his soul. I would see him at parties constantly stroking the egos of the guys in charge of recruitment. It was one of the most pitiful things I've ever seen. I felt sorry for the guy. They finally relented because they probably felt sorry for him, too. Then, once he was in and was given status, he became arrogant. His significance was completely based on his ability to exclude others from the "in crowd."

I ran into this guy a few years ago and the first thing to come out of his mouth was, "I can still take you," as if physically dominating me would be the quickest way to being respected. If we were a pack of wild dogs, I might agree. It seems when we are scared we revert to survival instincts. It was obvious that behind the scenes was a wounded little boy looking for meaning and trying to prove to the big scary world he's strong.

03. RELATIONSHIPS

I would imagine the famous line in *Jerry McGuire*, "You complete me," has probably wrecked more well-intentioned people than just about anything else. If you dissect this Hail Mary grasp at intimacy, it is essentially saying that he is broken and she is the only thing on the planet that can make him whole. I'm no math guy, but I do know if you add a negative number to another negative number, you just end up with a bigger negative. When you add a broken person to another broken person, you don't end up with two whole people. To say a fallible person will make you whole is to require that person to be perfect, but there is only One who is perfect.

I have another term for the phrase, "You complete me." It's called codependency. Codependency is a sneaky devil that masquerades as romance or even friendship but, at its core, it's needy, desperate, and self-serving. It will say anything it can to hook you, using all types of hidden manipulation motivated by the longing to connect. The truth is, the codependent person does not view himself or herself as worthy of love, and has his/her self esteem constantly on trial.

I think everyone has a certain degree of codependency. Unless we have had someone model healthy relationships for us or teach us how to have them, we will lean towards codependency. The reason it's so deadly is because, In its simplest form, codependency is putting people In the place of God. A way to know if this is affecting you is to do a self check: if you feel utter devastation versus ecstatic elation from someone's rejection versus acceptance of you, you may have a problem.

If that is the case for you, the first thing you need to do is dethrone that individual. Recognize we can't get all of our sense of worth from other people. It isn't fair to anyone involved. It's your job, no one else's, to recognize the tremendous value you carry. Can you imagine if people were actually honest with their pick up lines? "Hey listen, I don't really love myself. Can you be God for me and be responsible for convincing me I'm worthy of love?" Wow, that's a lot of pressure.

The second thing you need to do is to love yourself. God says we love because He first loved us.[5] God is the beginning of love. If we are to love our neighbors as ourselves, the way Jesus commanded, the first thing we need to do is to love ourselves well. Loving yourself isn't arrogant; it's a commandment. If we are going to love ourselves well, we need to first ask God to show us what He sees in us that is worthy of love. When we see ourselves as He sees us, we can love ourselves in a healthy way and give that love to others.

04. WEALTH

Jesus talked more about money than any other topic. Sixteen of His 38 parables were concerned with how to handle money and possessions. In the Gospels, an amazing one out of ten verses (288 in all) deal directly with the subject of money. The Bible overall offers 500 verses on prayer, less than 500 verses on faith, but more than 2,000 verses on money and possessions!

Why do you think this is? I think it's probably because God knew humanity would have the greatest tendency to put faith in something visible like money over an invisible God. Jesus said, "No one can serve two masters. Either you will hate the one and love the other, or you will be devoted to the one, and despise the other. You cannot serve both God and money."[6]

There was a dude—a king—in the Old Testament named Solomon who was the richest man probably to ever live. At the end of his life, he wrote about how he had done everything pos-

---

5   *John 4:19, NKJV*
6   *Matthew 6:24, ESV*

sible to try and see what would bring joy to humanity. There was no pleasure from which he withheld himself. But the final result was that he ultimately found that all of it was vanity and like "trying to catch the wind."[7] Despite giving himself entirely to the pleasure of what his riches provided him, it didn't make him happy in the core of who he was. It's the same reason the richest men in the world all seem to be making vows to give away their riches to create a better world. Because, past a certain point, money won't make you any happier.

You may be thinking: *Not a chance; if I had more money, I would be SO HAPPY.* Well, according to a study done by Princeton University, to a certain degree it will. The study says after someone makes more than $75,000 a year, overall satisfaction does not continue to go up. After spending years working in an industry that pays its employees hundreds of thousands of dollars a week, I can say from experience, It DOESNT make you happier. But while wealth does create a sense of safety, it will not satisfy your core needs for joy. That will have to come from within you by making the decision to be content. If you are constantly striving to create your nest egg, you will find yourself burnt out, stressed out, and alone. Ultimately, what will give you joy is knowing how much God loves you, and passing on that love to as many people as you can.

I was on a flight a few years ago and saw some football players gambling on the plane. As I was watching, I overheard them talking about how much they were going to bet on a college

---

7   *Ecclesiastes 2:11, NKJV*

football game. I heard them say, "How 'bout a hunnid?" I was surprised, thinking, *Wow, a hundred bucks is a lot to gamble.* It turned out they were talking about 100K! (I threw up in my mouth slightly over it.)

Over the years, I would see dozens of guys blowing through their money as if it would never stop. They would give themselves to the game so they could earn as much money as possible because having money in a bank account was a quick way to feel powerful. I even saw one guy bring his banker from Chase around with him—the teller from the bank, with the Chase logo on his necktie. This young man, hungry for significance, looked across the landscape of society for anyone he could align himself with to show the world he had arrived. He never will with a strategy like that.

I heard a story about one player who, each time he would get a massage from a lady before games, he would throw the money he owed her on the floor instead of handing it to her. He wanted to demonstrate that he was the one in charge, and he used his money to dominate people.

The last two seasons I played for the Seahawks, I started saving all of the per diem the team gave me for road games, in cash. When Matti and I decided to move back to Texas, I opened my stash to put the money towards our upcoming move. As I sat in my office with 100-dollar bills all over the floor, I couldn't help but feel powerful. It was intoxicating to actually see the money I had. I started to feel uneasy with that

WE LOVE BECAUSE

HE FIRST LOVED US.

feeling, so I took it to the bank and deposited it. I can see why Jesus said the love of money is the root of all kinds of evil. Ultimately, money just becomes a magnifier of who you are. There is nothing wrong with having money; just make sure money doesn't have you.

05. DRUGS AND ALCOHOL

If you want to find out the emotional state of our world, just take a look at how these substances are abused. While they make big promises of belonging and comfort, the false sense of well being will continue to produce diminished returns. As a young person, I battled with both drugs and alcohol all while genuinely wanting to live a life I would be proud of. I would find myself in overwhelming circumstances of anxiety, depression, or trauma, desperately turning to God, but feeling like, no matter how hard I prayed, the comforter continued to show up as a substance rather than a Spirit. I hated it and needed God's tenderness to deliver me from crippling fear.

When under the influence of drugs or alcohol, pain is numbed and confidence is bolstered. With each inducement of false confidence, the frequency and amount needed to sustain the effect increase. In our culture of instant gratification, we fail to realize that by continuing to kick the can down the road without dealing with our underlying pain, our actions will actually produce a great deal more pain in the long run. The best time to deal with your pain is now.

---

9   *Proverbs 27:7, NKJV*

There is a verse in the Bible that says, "To a hungry soul, every bitter thing is sweet."[8] In other words, if you have an ache needing soothing, you will have a propensity to consume low-level slop for sustenance. But even through all that, God doesn't hate you for your hunger. In fact, the state of your soul is a top priority to Him.

When your soul hungers, don't feed it with spiritual junk food full of empty promises; feed it with what it's really after—a spiritual experience surrounded by authentic and loving community. The opposite of addiction is not sobriety, it's connection. Keep that in mind if someone you love battles with these issues.

06. FAME

I think this idol might be the most insidious one of all. As I've mentioned, everyone wants to be significant—to be loved and have their lives matter. I have no issue with a healthy desire for that. However, things get tricky in the social media age we live in where followers are more of a ranking system than anything else. As I was researching this area, I found an article that gives a step-by-step guide on how to become famous. In a matter of weeks, this article had over 400,000 views.

I have a friend who is a youth pastor at a great church in Seattle. Their church is doing amazing things in the world and, since becoming a pastor there, he has become somewhat Instagram famous in the church scene. I was having breakfast with him one time and he told me, "Clint, it's so weird; I can't believe all the guys I know who are jealous because I have a couple thousand followers. The only thing these guys want is to be Instagram famous." He went on to tell me about an article he read that said one out of three college students in 2016 believed he or she would be famous someday.

Social media massages our ego and injects us with instant significance. Every time someone engages with us on social media, our brain pumps out the pleasure chemical called dopamine, actually creating a chemical dependence to our need for meaning. Social media isn't what birthed mankind's desire to be worshiped; it just gave us another tool.

I am thankful God got a hold of my heart before I got into the NFL. I see so many young guys come into the league not knowing who they are. On the outside they look like they have it all together but, in reality, they are scared, broken kids. Some of the most insecure people I know are professional athletes. I believe the reason many of them are there is because, as children, their coaches, parents, and fans would love and affirm them when they played well and withdrew from them when they didn't play well. You learn pretty quickly as a child that if you want to get your basic need for love met, trying hard in football is one of the quickest routes.

I had a coach tell me one time how easy it is to brainwash children. With a snicker he said, "Make them perform for love." Unfortunately, that was exactly how he coached, too. He produced great athletes and terribly broken men. It's no wonder that, in a few years after being out of their sport, many players turn to drugs and alcohol and blow through their money. Fame doesn't actually make you happy. In fact, the celebrity culture we have created may be one of the biggest destroyers of happiness our nation has.

07. YOUR FAVORITE SPORTS TEAM

I remember being on a bus with the Seahawks driving into Candlestick Park to play the 49ers in a Thursday night prime time game. The busses were full of energy as the players slowly bobbed their heads to the beats of their own headphones. I glanced out the window at a dad walking into the parking lot with his two young sons. They couldn't have been older than ten. I smiled, thinking how cool it was to see this dad investing time into his boys. As we drove past, the father began screaming all kinds of profanities at our bus right in front of his kids. He lifted up his hands demonstrating to his children the proper way to give the middle finger to the opposing team. His kids followed suit! This was his temple, and we weren't about to come in and rob him of the joy his god gave him. My smile faded—how sad!

In the Old Testament, you can see different accounts of how people would worship the creation rather than the Creator. The first thing they would do was find some type of mascot, like maybe a Bear (Chicago), or a bird (Seattle Seahawks), or a fish (Florida Marlins) that would represent their strength. Then would they would paint their faces, make a flag, put on their clothes (like maybe a jersey) that symbolized their mascot, and go out to war. *Sound familiar?*

How often do you see all of these things at a sporting event, even to the extent where people compare a football game to warfare? I have nothing against sports, obviously, but it's a terrible religion. If you win, the whole city loves you; if you lose, well, God just died. I would see people worshiping their favorite athletes and as soon as that person wasn't perfect (because we must have a god who is perfect), they demonized him. The 19th century preacher Jonathan Edwards said it best, "If you idolize it, you will demonize it."

I remember January 10, 2016 when the Seahawks were in a playoff game against the Minnesota Vikings. It went down as the third coldest game in NFL history. The temperature was negative six degrees but there was a wind chill factor of negative 25. It was so cold that the moisture in my breath began to freeze my eyelashes together.

As I ran out for the first punt snap of the game, I could hardly feel my hands. When I gripped the ball, it felt like an ice cube. I threw the ball with all my might and it resulted in the worst snap I have ever had. The ball bounced back and caused our punter to have to try and scramble for the first down. He ended up breaking his nose in the process and cost our team three points. Thankfully, at the end of the game, their kicker missed the game-winning kick and bailed me out. But I was still the most hated man in Seattle.

Even though it ultimately didn't cost us the game, people were insanely angry. I got voicemails, Tweets, Instagram comments, and Facebook comments all saying how I was the worst per-son ever. On top of that, the following day in our team meet-ing, I was crucified in front of the whole team and shamed over how horrible of a snap it was. It was one of the most humiliating moments of my life.

But how ridiculous is that? I mean, I realize winning in the NFL means money. But was I really the worst person in the world? Like more than Hitler? Of course not, but when people find out the thing they are attaching all of their hope to has failed them, they freak out. That's idolatry, plain and simple.

GOT IDOLS? YOU'RE NOT ALONE

If you felt a stirring in your heart reading about any of the above idols, you are not alone and you are not bad! Everyone has appetites we are trying to get filled just to survive. All of humanity is broken—it's not just you. But broken people will ultimately break other people. When the people in your world don't esteem you, it makes it tough to love yourself, especially if you don't realize just how accepted you are to God.

That's what causes us to look for identity and comfort in the creation, instead of in our Creator. Our fallen nature opens us up to being wounded by the people we hold in high es-teem. But if we look beyond the superficial, what do all of our idols ultimately promise? They offer significance, safety, and/

or comfort—all things God promises to give us when we turn to Him and place Him first in our lives.

Friends, we need to get our wounds healed and our needs met in the proper way. If we don't, we'll carry wounds of rejection around our whole lives. We'll be constantly feeding on spiritual junk food that satiates just enough to keep our pain from killing us and our tears from drowning us. All the while, God is waving His hands trying to show us a better way and promising to take what was meant for harm and make it work out in our favor.[9]

Even after I had turned my life over to God, I found myself in the cycle of idolatry, going back and forth between false comforts and false fathers. I was still trying to cover pain that had not been totally healed yet. It can be so frustrating to find yourself stuck in patterns you want to be out of, and feeling like you keep fighting the same battles, year after year. It's even more frustrating when everyone around you seems to expect you to have it all together. Trust me, I get it.

So here is some advice: give yourself a break. God knew what He was getting into when He reached down into your life. He isn't surprised at your humanity and He is definitely not in a hurry. Wholeness is an onion we will continue to peel away, one layer at a time. In the meantime, love the process.

---

9   *Romans 3:23*

"You matter to me." - God

BREAKING FREE

There is a story of an executive who was busy working in his home office when his six-year-old son came in asking him to play. After much persistence, followed by much frustration, the exec pulled out a magazine and opened it to a large foldout map of the world. Pulling out the map, he cut it into a whole bunch of tiny pieces and gave them to his son. "Here, son, after you put together this map of the world, then I'll play with you." Knowing a six-year-old has no idea what a map of the world looks like, he assumed this task should keep his son busy for at least a couple hours.

But ten minutes later, his son came back into the office and said, "All done, Daddy." The executive thought his son was exaggerating; but upon going into the living room, he found the entire map perfectly assembled.

"Son, how on Earth did you figure out how to do this so quickly?" he asked incredulously.

"It was easy, Daddy." The boy began turning over the pieces one at a time, and as he did, his father saw that a photograph of a man was on the other side of the world map. "You see, Daddy, when you put the man together, the whole world falls into place."

The first step towards seeing the world around you at peace is recognizing we do actually need to be put back together. All

---

10   Proverbs 23:7

of us have sinned, and "fall short of the glory of God."[10] Or, as the New Living Translation of the Bible says it, " . . . we all fall short of God's glorious standard."

Until you know how far God went to bring you back into relationship with Him, to bring you up to His "glorious standard," you will never be able to quiet the voices of rejection that cause you to turn to addictive garbage when you feel hungry for love. You see, God steps down into our world and says, "You matter to me." When the world tells you that you are not enough, God says, "You don't have to perform for Me." When you don't know who you are, God says, "I will tell you who you are." Rejection comes when identity is not imparted and God is a master at doing just that— imparting identity.

Every person has moments when he or she feels the world is asking him (or her) to be something he (or she) is not entirely sure is possible. All of us ask ourselves the questions, *Do I have what it takes? Am I powerful? Am I enough?* You don't have to go very far to find a voice causing you to doubt your value. I mean, if people rejected Jesus, who was perfect, you probably are going to be confronted with it, too!

I hope you will allow God to be on the throne of your heart and give you His perspective. All rejection is simply negative judgment, and all judgment is subjective information by nature. This means you have the power to interpret people's rejection as their perception and not as a result of anything wrong with you.

---

11   *Proverbs 27:3*

The Bible says, "For as a man thinks in his heart, so is he."[11] You are what you believe about yourself. If you continue to believe you are rejected, you will continue to fall into the traps of idols and subconsciously look for evidence of it. Here is the truth: you are not rejected. What person on Earth has the audacity to assume he or she has the power to reject what Christ has accepted? No one!

Does this mean you will never feel the sting of rejection? That's doubtful. But when you see yourself as Christ sees you and you become aware of the magnificence in you that God thought was worth dying for, rejection begins to lose its sting.

I spent so much of my life looking to earn the approval of men whom I saw as powerful, but whom, ultimately, I didn't have any desire to model my life after. I lifted coaches, teachers, and friends up to a higher place than God in my eyes, and they could single-handedly ruin me or cause me to thrive. I hope you won't do that. If you allow people to have that sort of influence in your life, you have made them your God. When they fail, you, too will fall into the idol cycle *until you realize who you really are in Christ.*

HEALING FOR REJECTION

Here is a list of things to look out for. If you feel like any of these describe you, you might have an area of rejection that needs healing:

- [ ] Rebellion

- [ ] Fabricated personalities, faking who you are to be accepted

- [ ] Sabotaging relationships before people have a chance to reject you

- [ ] A pervasive wondering if someone likes you or is mad at you

- [ ] Feelings of not fitting in—a need to fit in or be a part of everything

- [ ] Self pity

- [ ] Inability to receive constructive criticism

- [ ] A tendency to blame God

- [ ] Arrogance

- [ ] Being opinionated

- [ ] Giving insincere compliments to gain favor

- [ ] Always needing to be right

- [ ] Asking permission when it's not required

- [ ] Feelings of worthlessness, insecurity, or hopelessness

- [ ] Approval-seeking

- [ ] Baiting people for compliments

- [ ] Envy, jealousy, or hate

- [ ] Fear of confrontation

- [ ] Fear of intimacy

- [ ] Addictions

If you see any of these things in yourself and think they may be rooted in rejection, I invite you to talk to God about them. To do that, you need to know what He's actually like. Having a right view of your Heavenly Father is a big deal. He is a loving Father who is waiting for you to come to Him with your needs and hurts so He can help and heal. Maybe you don't know Him yet or don't know much about Him. If that's you, allow me the pleasure of introducing you to Him.

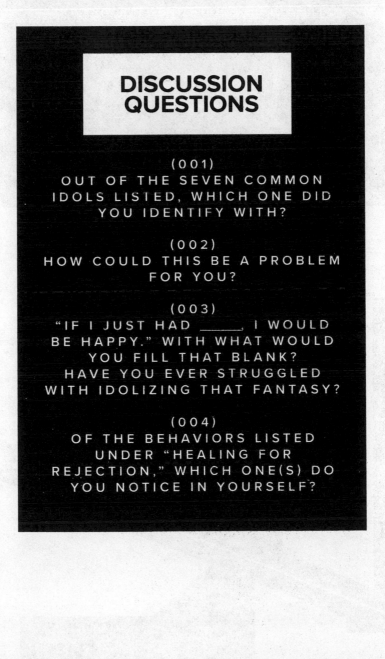

DISCUSSION QUESTIONS

(001)
OUT OF THE SEVEN COMMON IDOLS LISTED, WHICH ONE DID YOU IDENTIFY WITH?

(002)
HOW COULD THIS BE A PROBLEM FOR YOU?

(003)
"IF I JUST HAD _____, I WOULD BE HAPPY." WITH WHAT WOULD YOU FILL THAT BLANK?
HAVE YOU EVER STRUGGLED WITH IDOLIZING THAT FANTASY?

(004)
OF THE BEHAVIORS LISTED UNDER "HEALING FOR REJECTION," WHICH ONE(S) DO YOU NOTICE IN YOURSELF?

ABBA-LONG TO YOU

The second coolest experience I had as a professional athlete was when the Seahawks were invited to the White House to shake hands with the president (in celebration of winning the Super Bowl, which of course was the first coolest experience). It was a surreal moment.

The event was an all-day affair. After making it through multiple security checks, we were escorted to a waiting area to wait for the president. Dozens of dressed-up servers milled around with trays of drinks and snacks. A band played, and paintings of former presidents gave the distinct impression they still were watching over our nation and us. I think we all felt pretty special.

As we waited, everyone was taking pictures together. Even the guys usually too cool or too famous to ask for pictures joined in on the fun. It was a beautiful moment that turned about 100 full-grown men into boys—little boys with no titles, no fame, and no ego. We were just a bunch of guys sitting smack dab in the middle of their childhood dream.

When the president finally arrived, we all fell into a tight line to shake his hand one by one. Then we walked straight into a pressroom where he would address the nation with all of us standing proudly behind him. I don't know how it happened, but somehow I ended up in the front row just to the left of the president. Talk about prime real estate! (My mom always said I had a knack for being in the camera's eye.)

As the president began to address the nation about our spectacular season, I looked out into the sea of cameras. It seemed there were more cameras there than people! It was hard to wrap my mind around the idea that, although there were only about 200 people in the room, this event was going to be seen by millions of viewers.

You could tell President Obama had done his homework (or someone had). His entire speech included the perfect amount of honor, humor, and enthusiasm for football. Things were going great until about halfway in, when he began praising "the Legion of Boom," a name used to describe our defensive backfield. As the president mentioned the names of our four starting defensive backs, I realized he had gotten one of the names wrong. What? I couldn't believe it. How could he make a mistake like that? However, after thinking about it for a moment, I realized what had happened. One of the players in the "Legion of Boom," one of its founding members, so to speak, had to miss several games in the 2013-2104 season. Everyone had been shocked. We needed this guy! The LOB wasn't the same without him.

We ended up having another player come and fill in for him during the last stretch of the season and into the playoffs. But even though Brandon wasn't technically a part of the first Super Bowl in Seahawks history, he still played a massive role in getting us there. And even though he didn't play in the Super Bowl and wasn't even on our team at the time of meeting the president, he still deserved to be recognized as the fourth member of the ferocious unit.

With our eyes fixed and minds stunned, every single one of us faced the president with a smile on our faces, shocked over the misspoken words. I was bothered. In a moment, the greatest honor due to one person was given to someone else. It was like a little boy waiting for his dad to say "good job," but never hearing it.

While all this was going on, I noticed our head coach, a short space in front of me, glance up and give Brandon a head nod. It was a slight but powerful gesture, acknowledging, *Even when the most important person in the world disregards you, I still see you.*

Each and every one of us longs to be told, "I see you; I'm proud of you and you are valuable." When we don't hear that, especially at the times we need or want it most, it can feel painful and isolating. In that moment at the White House, a childlike glow of eager anticipation was snuffed out with just a few words. The President of the United States of America, the leader of the free world, unknowingly neglected a soul worthy and expectant of recognition. The ache of a heart looking for validation was palpable.

GETTING PAST WHAT OTHER PEOPLE THINK

Have you ever had someone you admire dismiss you? I don't think it matters if it's on purpose or not—it hurts all the same. Humans are not perfect and will let us down; that's a given. Consequently, all of us are going to experience feelings of abandonment and disappointment at one point or another in our lives. Many times, these feelings can be related to the father figures in our lives (biological dads, uncles, coaches, mentors, etc.). In the realm of professional football, for every one story from a teammate about his great, caring, and supportive dad, I could give you 100 filled with abuse, neglect, and apathy. The things some of my friends have had to fight through to make it to where they are today are nothing short of astounding. It makes me so grateful and appreciative of the family I have.

Football plays an interesting role for many of the guys. For most of them, it was their only shot at a better life: a ticket out of a certain neighborhood, fame, money, and a purpose in life. At an early age, these guys excelled. When they excelled, many of these boys who lived in a home void of love were abruptly thrust into a position where the better they played, the more praise and affirmation they received. Suddenly, a very normal human need for affection and love was filled. Football became the pseudo-savior of a longing boy's heart, because the harder he tried, the more love he was given.

For you, or for someone you know, it may not be football that fills this need; it may be something else. The brokenness we carry becomes the pistons that fire our motor towards greater and greater works. You see it in religion, sports performance, job performance, or even parenting, Wounds become warnings that sear themselves into our brains, never to be forgotten.

The "chip on the shoulder attitude" is oftentimes nothing more than admirably disguised pain many are too afraid to surrender. In essence, to forgive would decommission many top achievers' drive, and neuter their performance.

I remember hearing one particular press conference in which a player began to say how respected he felt after getting a big contract. In a way, the number tied to his contract wasn't a reflection of who he was as a football player but who he was as a man. He had bought the lie that what he *did* defined who he was.

While I understand the joy that comes when we work hard for something (all for it), to tether respect and love to our work or performance the way he did is a trap. The logic is flawed. Do the dollar signs next to someone's name somehow prove he is more worthy of love (and respect, support, affirmation, validation, etc.) than a single mom trying to feed her kids? Or a passionate teacher who makes 30 grand a year? Did Jesus die harder for this man than someone who isn't as successful publicly? Not a chance!

This performance mindset has become far too integrated in our culture. The sad thing is that this man will likely always make the people close to him perform for his love the way he always felt he had to. It's unavoidable, and it will be subtle. A look of disappointment or a tone of disgust will unconsciously communicate to his wife, his children, and anyone else he comes into contact with that if they want to get what they desperately need—unconditional love—they'd better walk on the eggshells he has placed in front of them precisely the way he expects. This further perpetuates the conditional love he was given—the love on a sliding scale that echoes, *What have you done for me lately?*

God gave us a perfectly normal desire for affection and affirmation. But apart from understanding the love of the Heavenly Father, it can get twisted. The cycle works like this: you do good things, people tell you how great you are, and you begin to believe those good things make you worthy of love. You get elated when you receive attention but become depressed and rejected when you don't. With performance comes the possibility of failure, and to fail means you aren't worthy of love.

As I was getting ready for the NFL scouting combine my rookie year, I remember stumbling onto the verse, "The fear of man brings a snare, but whoever trusts in the Lord shall be safe."[12]

---

12   *Proverbs 29:25*

PEOPLE BOUND WITH THE FEAR OF MAN THINK PEOPLE ARE BIGGER THAN GOD.

#BECOMINGBOOK

Little did I know this verse would be a life anchor for me rather than simply a poetic nicety to recite as 32 NFL special teams coaches stared me down while assigning my value.

You see, as I mentioned earlier, I used to really, really care about what other people thought of me. The Bible calls this "the fear of man." My entire sense of worth was based on either the warmth or the iciness I felt from other people. It was exhausting to always be living in other people's heads. *What are they thinking about me? What are they saying about me?* People bound with the fear of man think people are bigger than God. They esteem other people's critique, affection, and attention with the highest importance. When you regard man more than God, you will sell your soul to get the affection you crave.

At the combine, I spent the four-day process doing all sorts of things: interviews, personality questionnaires, leg strength machines, drug tests, and so on. I was constantly evaluated with questions like, "What are you eating? Who are you talking to? Are you in a good mood?" If there was ever a time I needed to trust God and not "fear man," it was then.

During the interviews, I came across a special teams coach who made some disparaging comments that I wasn't big enough. For years, I have had a difficult time adding mass to my frame. It seems like a contrary problem to have but it's been troubling for me. I just can't seem to put pounds on.

The remarks from the special teams coach stuck with me. With my inability to add healthy weight, I was constantly afraid I wasn't going to be heavy enough. If I wasn't heavy enough, I wouldn't be able to block; if I couldn't block, I couldn't do my job; if I couldn't do my job, I might get cut from a team; if I get cut from a team and I'm no longer a football player . . . well, there goes my identity. It's amazing how codependency, which is based on lies, can become rooted into real life issues!

My weight problem got to the point of trying ridiculous things to stay heavy. When I became part of the Seahawks team, they would monitor each player's weight weekly. Wednesday mornings, right after special teams meetings, I would head into the weight room where a coach would have me hop on the scale so he could fill out his weight report. It was always a stressor for me. Each trip to the scale was a moment where time stopped, and I held my breath in hopes I would be big enough and, in my mind, good enough. The number 240 was seared into my mind as the threshold of being good or bad; if my weight was 240 pounds or above, I would receive a smile and a nod of approval that would leave me feeling like I was invincible (for a few hours). But at 239.9, I would receive a verbal thrashing.

Fear is a powerful motivator, but usually results in diminishing returns. I eventually realized that one bottle of water equated to about one pound. So, for a long time, I would chug two or three water bottles before our special teams meeting every

Wednesday. This seemed like a great idea until about 8:30 am when all of that water would hit me. My bladder would be so full I couldn't even lean forward in my seat! As soon as that meeting was finished, I would waddle to the weigh-in room before sprinting to the bathroom. It was a photo finish each time.

As time went on, I began to feel convicted about it. At the end of the day, I was deceiving my boss. My integrity was on the line. In addition to that (and what I believe was the bigger issue), I was allowing a root of fear to continue to take up mental territory in my head instead of driving those defeating thoughts out like I should have.

In some ways, it wasn't a huge deal. People weren't going to die because I lied to my strength coach about how heavy I was. No one was going to lose any sleep—no one except for me, that is. The Bible says when you handle the small situations of life with integrity, God can trust you to not lose sight in the big situations. God has a habit of sprinkling these seemingly inconsequential opportunities to choose integrity all throughout our lives. My weight challenge was one of mine—and I was blowing it.

When I think back on low moments of juggling so much pressure, I feel sorry for choosing fear. I'm sorry I did that, and I would never do it now. As they say, hindsight is 20/20! I've learned, instead of lambasting ourselves with sternness, self compassion is the only way to grow from any disappointment. But while I'm frustrated over the failure, it also was a good learning experience for me. It brought me to the realization that I obviously didn't see God as big enough, powerful enough, or loving enough to help me through that situation legitimately. I didn't really know my Heavenly Father.

HOW WE SEE HIM MATTERS

When you think of God the Father, what comes to mind? Did you know that how we view God is the most influential belief when it comes to our worldview? For example, I don't really like spending time with people who don't like me (who does?). So, if I think God is consistently irritated with me, I most likely won't want to spend much time with Him. On the other hand, if I understand how much He likes me, I will enjoy a deep and satisfying relationship with Him.

To live out our true identity as a son or daughter of God, we need to ask ourselves what we actually believe about His character. Here are five common ways people view God:

01. GENIE

The individual with this view is most likely a Type A personality. He or she is likely accomplished, esteemed, and driven, and is looking for a competitive edge. Think of the professional athlete who prays before a game for success, then spends the rest of his week building his kingdom rather than God's Kingdom. He would never admit it, but this person is insecure and hides behind his accomplishments. He will give a nod to God, but it comes from a place of superstition and selfishness rather than a heart to know his Heavenly Father.

02. FIRE TRUCK

This type of belief seems to be the most prevalent in the Church, and can be characterized as the "lukewarm believer." This person does not live a life surrendered to Jesus but believes he or she is doing better than the person next to him (or her). She will go to church on holidays and pray before meals, but her inner world has not seen a radical transformation by the Love of God. This person wants God far away for most of her life, but, when she is in trouble, she wants Him to get there fast.

03. TORMENTOR

This view of God is most prevalent in people who are either agnostic (think there could be a higher power) or atheist (believe there is no God). These people attribute all the evil of the world to God. They hang their distrust of God on questions like, "Why do bad things happen to good people?" and, "Why does God send people to hell?" They believe God is in the clouds playing roulette with their lives, as if their destruction and/or suffering are a source of sick pleasure. They believe you should be suspicious of people who say they serve God.

04. TASKMASTER

This person means well but always seems to find himself or herself burnt out or under extremely heavy condemnation. He sees God as a Great King who is so high above him he is not

worthy to interact with Him. There is a strong likelihood this person was shamed a great deal as a child and has a very low sense of self worth. He feels like a slave constantly trying to earn the approval of a disappointed and aloof hero. He is easily offended when he sees real intimacy with God. On a subliminal level, his holiness is based on how good or bad the people around him are. I usually hear these kinds of people talking about "suffering" for Christ quite a bit, as if that is the number one metric for holiness. This person furrows his brow at Jesus' words, "No longer do I call you servants, for a servant does not know what his master is doing; but I have called you friends."[13] At the end of the day, this person does not believe he is worthy of love. Receiving love with no strings attached is the most uncomfortable thing in the world. This person will always be looking to either repay favors or subconsciously sabotage and push away real intimacy and friendship.

05. PAPA

The person with this worldview is at peace with God and the world around her. She has fostered a deep relationship with God in what Psalm 91 calls "the secret place." At the end of the day, this person has moved from praying for what is on her heart to discussing it with her Dad in Heaven, and hearing what is on His heart. When she loves other people, she does it without needing anything in return because she is so secure in her identity and worth. She has courageously allowed God into the darkest most broken areas of her heart. She is not perfect, but people who live in the other categories may see

---

13   *John 15:15, NKJV*

her as perfect and confident. She still has insecurities and doubts but chooses to bring them into the light of God and community rather than pretend she has it all together.

As I was writing this, I realized that, at any given moment, I can find myself drifting through any five of these beliefs about God. No one is immune to viewing God inaccurately at times. The bombardment of worldly messages (especially in TV, movies, and magazines), spiritual attacks, and our own warped appetites can make even the most devout follower of Jesus bend under the weight of pride, exasperation, or fear.

If you are a follower of Jesus, you need community and God's Word to guide you in life and to help keep you on the right path. God is not looking for perfection or minions; He's simply looking for friends who will choose a transparent relationship with Him.

STEPPING UP MY GAME

At the end of each NFL season, you sit down with your position coach and recap how things went over the last 17 weeks. You will set some goals and take a look at your performance, the good and the bad.

The Seahawks always did such a great job of empowering their players for growth and I was excited for another off-season full of improving myself. However, when I got home after my last exit meeting, the familiar feeling of conviction bubbled to the surface. I knew there was something I needed to address inside of me. I had this overwhelming impression that if I didn't deal with this spirit of fear motivating me, it would torment me the rest of my life. I needed a God bigger than any coach, teammate, friend, relationship, or even a Super Bowl to set me free from this fear. I needed my Father in Heaven to show me I was His son.

There is no greater voice in shaping the self worth of a young person than that of a father. A father imparts identity to his children so, when they go into the world, they live with the assurance they are loved and valuable. I needed a supernatural revelation of exactly how my Heavenly Father saw me. I was so tired of getting beat up with anxiety over what people thought of me. I was ready to fully and completely believe I belong to Him and to place my identity in Him alone.

One night, while reading my Bible, I landed in the book of Luke and found myself reading the story of the time Jesus fasted for 40 days. At the end of the story, the voice of the God speaks to Jesus saying, "You are My beloved Son, in whom I am well pleased." He wasn't pleased in Jesus because Jesus fasted; He was pleased because that's what a father is with his children. I wanted that kind of clarity in hearing the Father's voice! But as I look back on my weight anxieties, I know back then I didn't fully understand what God thought about me. I had picked up a performance mindset that kept me in a cycle of shame and insecurity. I felt like I needed to constantly be striving. While I wanted to have integrity, I didn't totally trust

God's character. I didn't believe, even if I fully trusted Him, that He would take care of me.

Fear had kept me safe through the years from that big scary world full of people who could hurt me. In a twisted way, the spirit of fear had become my friend—in the way alcohol is a friend to an alcoholic. The unspoken agreement between my fear addiction and me was, *If you keep me safe, I will give you a home.* I fed that spirit (fear), catered to it, obeyed it, and was tortured by it. It kept me safe in a cage of isolation—a cage void of the embrace of my Father's love. I needed out of that cage— and I was willing to do just about anything to gain my freedom.

THE ROAD TO FREEDOM

In Jentezen Franklin's book, *Fasting*, he talks about taking a season to deny your physical needs to give yourself a spiritual tune-up. I had tried fasting before, but I always felt closer to God while eating Chick-Fil-A. But I figured a little hunger was worth being free from fear.

Have you ever decided to do something before really counting the costs of the decision? Hypothetically, suppose you're a professional football player who is required to stay heavy and you decide to follow Jesus and do a 40-day fast? Yeah! After fasting two meals and only drinking liquids, I realized how much weight I was going to lose and started to panic. *This was a bad idea!*

THE ANTIDOTE TO *fear* ISN'T SAFETY BUT

COUR

AGE.

#BECOMINGBOOK

My old friend fear started whispering to me again. I heard it in-cessantly in the back of my mind, promising it could take care of me and keep me safe, whispering, *Come on, you're being way too intense about this stupid fast idea.* The diabolical thing about fear is that it masquerades as wisdom. It promises you safety, but what it really gives you is isolation. It gives full assurance of peace but riddles you with anxiety.

I can't think of a bigger enemy to courage than comfort. No-body has ever lived a fulfilling life without taking a single risk. Furthermore, if your Father in Heaven really promises He works all things out for your good,[14] is there really such a thing as failure? I knew that stopping my fast would be more com-fortable. But that was not the courageous call.

I was faced with another one of those seemingly inconsequen-tial decisions. Would I trust the familiar voice of fear or would I trust that my Father in Heaven knows me and sees me? The "what ifs" were strong: *What if I lose too much weight? What if I'm not ready when I get back to football? What if the Sea-hawks cut me because I'm too small? What will they think of God since they know I'm a Christian and I'm not ready to do my job?* I pictured the Father in Heaven wringing His hands, worrying as much as I was. That image seemed ridiculous.

I sensed a knowing smile and a loving tone say, "You'll be okay." I guess you decide to be brave before you actually feel like you are.

---

14   *Romans 8:32*

About three weeks into my fast, I went down to visit a friend of mine who was in his second year at a ministry school connected to a church in California. This church had been a huge influence on my life for years, and I was so excited to get to go to a few classes with my friend and experience the culture around campus.

One of the things they did an amazing job with was prayer. Small groups gather to pray for individuals with specific needs for God's mercy and encouragement. They listen for the voice of God's Spirit and share whatever they receive. People often weep for joy over how God uses total strangers to speak what they really need to hear!

That evening, I went with my buddy Kevin to a friend's house where they were having a time of this prayer ministry. It was eventually my turn, so I sat down in a chair as a few of his friends prayed for me. A couple minutes into the prayer time, a girl said to me, "I sense the Father wants to teach you about your identity. He says you are His son, and He is pleased in you." Wow, that really got my attention!

But get this: the next day, while I was walking around the church, I had a total stranger walk up to me and say, "Hey, this may sound weird, but I feel like God wants to tell you your identity is in Him." *Okay, God, I am listening now.*

This church has a 24-hour prayer room available for anyone to go inside. I decided I was going to use it, and planned to stay up all night and ask God to heal the areas where my identity was not settled. Around three o'clock in the morning, I felt like God wanted to give me three specific verses to focus on regarding identity. While searching for the final verse in my Bible, the story crossed my mind of Jesus being baptized and the voice of the Father saying, "This is My beloved Son, in whom I am well pleased."

Now, even though this verse was the one that, in a way, had inspired my fast, the more I thought about it the more I felt like it wasn't for me. This wasn't because I didn't think it was a great verse about identity. I felt I needed Him to tell me something more specifically about *me*. I think part of me hoped to stumble upon a new book in the Bible where God would speak my name and reveal His plan for me—a presumptuous idea, but that's how desperate I was.

After a few more minutes of prayer, I employed the old point and shoot tactic—the one where you close your eyes, open up your Bible, and randomly place your finger on the page hoping you land on just the right passage. I opened my eyes and found myself in 2 Peter 1:16-18. What I found blew my mind:

> *For we did not follow cunningly devised fables when we made known to you the power and coming of our Lord Jesus Christ, but were eyewitnesses of His majesty. For He received from God the Father honor and glory when such a voice came to Him from the Excellent Glory: 'This is My beloved*

Son, in whom I am well pleased.' And we heard this
voice which came from heaven when we were with
Him on the holy mountain. (NKJV)

I was in total shock. This was the verse I originally heard but had disregarded. The passage goes on to say no scripture is of any private interpretation. I take that to mean God's Word applies to everyone. What God said to Jesus, He is also saying to me. The moment was so holy for me, and so evident of God's fingerprint, I shuddered in reverence.

The Creator—the One who made oxygen, mountains, and breakfast burritos—was communing with me. Me! The kid who thought he had every reason in the world to not be worthy of love, the kid who had jumped through so many religious hoops trying to earn the attention of God, the kid who feared so much what everyone else thought of him. In that moment, my Heavenly Father whispered (or maybe He shouted) He loved me. He was pleased with me. I had heard that verse a thousand times. But until I had God open up my heart to see it, It never stuck. Sometimes life's crucial messages are not in the new things we learn but in remembering the things we already know.

In that moment, I was forever changed. I had heard a voice of approval that wasn't connected to my performance. But you know what? SometImes, even now, I still have moments where I feel like that kid looking for approval. Sometimes I am unsure whether the things I do are any good. I wonder if the people

MY SELF WORTH IS ANCHORED IN WHO GOD SAYS I AM, NOT PEOPLE.

clapping for me would really like me if they got to know me. I take comfort in the realization that everyone feels like that from time to time. If someone tells you they don't have these little insecurity gremlins whisper in their ear occasionally, he (or she) is lying. (If I ever do meet someone who doesn't hear this kind of stuff in their mind, you'd better believe I'm going to get them to pray for me!)

STEPPING OUT OF THE BOAT—AND INTO HIS ARMS

The antidote to fear isn't safety but courage. We each play a part in our own story of redemption by stepping out of the boat when the Father calls our name.

For some, the phrase "father" has a negative connotation. It brings up feelings of abandonment or disappointment for many of us. However, in the Bible the word for father is *Abba*. Jesus uses the term once in the book of Mark and Paul uses it once each in Romans and Galatians. *Abba* is a term that means "Papa" or "Daddy." Interestingly, the biblical writers employed a word conveying a childlike innocence rather than using the word "father." It would seem, then, that the relationship Jesus invites us into with Abba is not one that is merely positional or steeped in stoicism but a tender relationship full of acceptance and free of striving and shame.

This is the kind of father experience my teammate Brandon had that day when President Obama inadvertently failed to mention him. As soon as the president finished mentioning the LOB, Coach Carroll slowly turned his head and looked straight at Brandon. Their eyes locked and Coach gave Brandon a nod. Brandon nodded right back. Although Brandon didn't get the recognition he'd hoped for, a father figure stepped in and Brandon heard him clearly: *You matter; I see you and you are worthy of recognition.*

Are you looking for the approval of someone? I have been down the road of approval-seeking far too often. I have exchanged my authenticity for the hit of dopamine I got when parents, coaches, teachers, or anyone cooler than me acknowledged me.

There are likely people in your life you are desperate to receive approval from. I hate to break it to you, but you may never get it. Not only that, if it's beating you up that badly, this person may well have taken the place of God in your life.

What do you do when the most important person in your world fails to acknowledge you? When that happens, your Father in Heaven is standing close by looking you straight in the eye and telling you that, even though the rejection may sting, He sees you—and you're still so important to Him.

DISCUSSION QUESTIONS

(001)
WHY ARE FATHERS SO IMPORTANT
IN OUR LIVES?

(002)
WHAT WAS/IS YOUR FATHER LIKE?

(003)
HOW HAS YOUR RELATIONSHIP WITH
YOUR DAD INFLUENCED YOUR VIEW
OF GOD?

(004)
WHAT DO YOU SENSE GOD WANTING
TO SAY TO YOU TODAY ABOUT YOUR
RELATIONSHIP WITH HIM?

PIZZA FOR THE SOUL

Since as far back as I can remember, validation from women has been really important to me. I was always that kid showing off in front of the girls in playground.

In 1993, when *Jurassic Park* came out, I was able to claw myself to the top as the leader of the Saint James Episcopal school raptor club. This was a real life club where my friends and I would run around the playground, high-stepping and throwing our feet out in front us, pretending we were velociraptors with huge talons on our feet. It was serious business being the focus of the female raptors on the playground.

But what was just fun for everyone else during recess had a much deeper meaning to me. The disastrous freshman year date I mentioned in chapter one shows I struggled when relating to the opposite sex. Relationships were an idol for me because of the sense of satisfaction I got when I knew a girl admired me. I loved that someone liked me. I needed it mostly because I didn't like myself. I would do whatever I could to get someone to like me, even if it meant saying things I didn't mean. But under that desperate teen angst was another, more sobering, truth.

YOUR BRAIN ON LOVE

Have you ever known someone with an addiction? I don't mean like going back for seconds on dessert but a real addiction? It can be exhausting.

While I was playing for the Seahawks, the NFL would bring speakers to come in and talk to the teams about all kinds of different issues. One day they brought in a former professional basketball player named Chris Herren who shared his story of addiction and the danger of substance abuse.

He told the story of how, while he was playing for the Boston Celtics, he was in the middle of pre-game warm ups when he learned his drug dealer was caught in traffic and couldn't get him the pills he needed. In full uniform, Chris walked out of the stadium and into traffic to get his pills. Our whole team was amazed at how far his addiction to drugs had taken him. As I sat there contemplating how ridiculous his story was, I had a revelation.

A year before this, I had gone on a few dates with a girl and had let my emotions get way ahead of me. She lived about three hours away by car, which meant we spent a bunch of time on the phone. After about a month of this, I felt those old feelings of codependency creeping up on me. I realized I was starting to get clingy. I felt like I was going crazy. I would call and wouldn't hear back for a week and had no idea why.

She finally texted me one Friday saying she would call me over the weekend, which I translated as, "You should drive down and visit me." So, I jumped in my car in the middle of rush hour to go see her. She didn't even know I was coming. Thankfully, after an hour of sitting in Seattle traffic and only moving about five miles, I realized how ridiculous I was being and turned around and went home.

Something was going on inside my brain, leading me to do ridiculous things just to see someone I cared about but barely knew. It was the same kind of drive that had led one of the top basketball players in the country out of a stadium in full uniform, in public, to score drugs. Our addictions roar for a fix and confuse our brains with irrational urgency, fear, and false promises of survival.

I recently stumbled upon an eye-opening Ted Talk by biological anthropologist Dr. Helen Fisher. Her studies found that, during brain scans, the same area of the brain that lights up while one is in love lights up when one feeds a cocaine addiction. Here is how it goes: let's say you develop a crush on someone in your third period chemistry class. Each time you see this person, you feel euphoric. You wanna know why? It's because your brain is pumping out enough dopamine (feel good chemical) to make Donald Trump want to hug Rosie

O'Donnell. Every time you think of your crush, your brain wants more. You begin to notice when your crush walks into the room—you sweat or your heart begins to race. That's because your brain has now signaled your adrenal glands to begin pumping out epinephrine, and norepinephrine. These are stress chemicals that make you do crazy things like when a grandma picks up a car to save a baby. It begins to give you a huge surge of excitement, making you more infatuated and obsessed. All reasoning has gone out the window and the primitive part of your brain has taken over.

Now you are hooked. All you want is to be around this person. Your brain craves the bath of chemicals it receives when you see him or her. The drive for love is actually stronger than the drive for sex; we crave it. So your limbic reward system continues to douse your brain with dopamine, which keeps you craving the object of your obsession. When that person is not around, you may start to have withdrawal symptoms, which drives you to manipulate circumstances in order to get to him or her again.

As you continue to fall in love, and your limbic reward system explodes like the Fourth of July; your amygdala begins to shut down. This can be a bad thing. You see, the amygdala, which is a set of neurons located in the temporal lobe, plays a big role in how we react to stimuli. It is critically important in helping us make judgment calls and recognize fearful situations. When this shuts down, we begin to gloss over shortcomings in our crush that are glaringly obvious to friends and family. As with any addiction, the high wears off and produces diminishing re-turns unless the person continues to reward your growing attachment.

If you continue to attach to this person, your brain will start to release oxytocin, which is nicknamed "the love hormone." This neuropeptide is produced in the hypothalamus and is released into our brains during intimate moments. It's actually the same hormone secreted when a mother breastfeeds her baby, or when orgasm happens. This hormone is hugely important to fostering trust and commitment. Unlike the quick high of dopamine, oxytocin is subtler, but lasts longer, leading to a deeper attachment.

Now all of this is wonderful when the person you're attaching to is the person to whom you are married. The problem happens when you get into this cycle and it isn't the time to be pursuing someone romantically, or when the person is not right for you. This was the state I perpetually found myself in. I was literally addicted to the rush of dopamine and endorphins that flooded my brain when I discovered chemistry between myself and someone else. There really wasn't much difference between me and the drug-addicted basketball player scoring drugs only minutes from tip-off. Both of us engaged in risky behavior for the sake of a high.

Our emotions are an incredibly powerful part of who we are. Unless we allow God to come into our lives and show us what real love looks like, we can find ourselves in a pretty bad situation, allowing our souls to attach to someone in a way God never intended.

What I realized was if I was going to be the man God wanted me to be, I needed to be at a place of wholeness. Love was my drug of choice to escape my feelings of inadequacy. But it really wasn't love at all; it was lust. We tend to confine lust to crude sexuality but it is much broader than that. Lust is simply selfish love. Love says give; lust says get. Lust will never be blessed by God, and it will create more pain than it will ever be worth. Jesus never modeled lust for us; He modeled unconditional love.

In John 13:34, Jesus said, "Let me give you a new command: Love one another. In the same way I loved you, you love one another" *(The Message)*. When I read this verse and looked at how Jesus expects us to love others, I realized how backwards I was. How did Jesus love? He loved extravagantly to the point of death. He loved people in the middle of their mess. He loved sacrificially. He knew who He was, and because of that, He could love others authentically without needing validation or affirmation in return. Jesus didn't mirror love given to Him; He was the source of it. He was the most non-codependent person to ever live. He was never intimidated by the shortcomings of others. He placed healthy boundaries on people, didn't allow people to walk all over Him, stood up for what was right, and stated His opinion, not fearing what people thought. He was full of the love of His Father; He never sacrificed His integrity to gain the love of others.

He loved his disciples *so well* that even when they abandoned Him He chose to love them. His continual demonstration of perfect love to a handful of rascally young men led a movement that has now impacted billions of people. Selfless love is powerful, and, until you have received it, you will never be able to give it.

LOVING SELFLESSLY

Have you ever told someone you loved them? I mean someone other than your parents, grandmother, or that delicious McDouble burger hand delivered by Ronald McDonald himself? I mean someone who wasn't required to love you back.

The first time I told a girl I loved her was terrifying. I was in middle school and it was thrown in at the bottom of an email. Middle school Clint was pretty rad and also pretty codependent. I had a wicked bowl cut, was into Korn, wore a puka shell necklace, and my screen name was sniper3522.

After the longest 25 minutes of my life, I finally got an email back. At the end of the email, she said those beloved words, "I love you." SCORE! Endorphin overload in this junkie's brain!

When I think back to this moment, I realize two things: one, I think she just liked me for my bowl cut, and two, if she hadn't reciprocated, "I love you," I would have been crushed.

I have had similar conversations that went the other way, too. You courageously step out of the boat hoping the water is going to hold under your feet, only to sink to the bottom of an ocean of rejection and embarrassment. There is nothing worse than telling someone how you feel and they tell you what a wonderful friend you are. And you think back, *Well, thankfully we are such great friends. Don't worry, I'll hold your purse for you while you go dance with that older guy who makes you feel insecure. He's perfect for you (CRYING).* Here's a shout out to all my fellow friend-zoned "nice guys!"

TYPES OF LOVE

In our society, the word "love" has become diluted and thrown around flippantly making once weighty, significant words trite. I love my wife, but I also love breakfast burritos. How is it I can use the same word for the woman I truly adore as I do about my favorite breakfast food? It makes no sense to me. But back in Jesus' day, they were clearer with their terms of endearment and had specific words to convey their measures of love.

One kind of love is called *eros* love. *Eros* is a Greek term that means "desire and longing." This kind of love has to do with sexuality and passion. If left to its own devices, separate from God and out of wedlock, it will lead to bondage because its first priority is to conquer and control.

The second kind of love the Bible talks about is called *phileo* love. This is a unique kind of love you would have with a close friend. (Think of Philadelphia, "The City of Brotherly Love.") This is the kind of love Jonathan and David had in the Old Testament. It is characterized by warmth.

I think this is where most of us land in our relationships with people we like. It can be shallow because It's the type of friendship that is often based on similarities, as opposed to a mature, conscious decision to love. It's your classic golfing buddy friendship. There's nothing wrong with it, but it is rooted in similar interests, social graces, and style. This love doesn't carry the type of weight Jesus wants us to walk in. It simply mirrors the love it receives.

The last kind of love Is called *agape*. There is nothing like this kind of love! When you know you are receiving it, it will shake you to the core. This is full-contact radical love, untethered by emotions but led by a decision that says, "I will seek your best interest no matter what you decide to do." It chooses to stay engaged in loving and is not dependent on actions from the other person. It's always on. And I think most people run from this type of love.

You may be thinking, *Why on earth would somebody run from being loved amazingly well?* Well, lets just say you are stuck in a season of feeling discouraged. You feel like you are going nowhere, doing nothing, and nobody cares. All of us have experienced seasons like this. Somebody comes along and thinks you are just great. The problem is that the script playing in the theatre of your mind is one of depression, discouragement, lack, fear, condemnation, and judgment. When a voice of love comes along and tells you something opposite of what the bombardment of accusations is telling you, it can make your head spin. Fear sets in. The fear is, *If you really knew me, you wouldn't love me. So I'd better keep you at a safe distance, because it's better to never let people close than to let them in only to be rejected by them.* Unfortunately, this mindset is all too common.

This *agape* love got me thinking one day. I knew this was the kind of love Jesus wanted me to demonstrate to people, but I didn't know how to do it. I decided I needed to find out for myself about what the Bible had to say about *agape*. What I found left me breathless.

I'M PETER

What comes to mind when you think of Peter the disciple? Is it his loud mouth? How he cut off an innocent man's ear? How he denied Jesus three times? Or maybe it's how he had a revelation that Jesus was the Christ. When I think about Peter, I can't help but relate to him. Peter loved Jesus but he was rough around the edges. He certainly didn't have it all figured out.

SELFLESS LOVE IS POWERFUL.

In my search for the word *agape* throughout Scripture, I found myself in Peter's story, in John 21, where it says:

> *So when they had eaten breakfast, Jesus said to Simon Peter, "Simon, son of Jonah, do you love Me more than these?"*
>
> *He said to Him, "Yes, Lord; You know that I love You."*
>
> *He said to him, "Feed My lambs." He said to him again a second time, "Simon, son of Jonah, do you love Me?"*
>
> *He said to Him, "Yes, Lord; You know that I love You."*
>
> *He said to him, "Tend My sheep." He said to him the third time, "Simon, son of Jonah, do you love Me?" Peter was grieved because He said to him the third time, "Do you love Me?"*[15]

At first glance, this doesn't really make sense. Jesus asks him three times whether he loves Him and the third time, Peter gets discouraged. Remember how I said our word for love has become diluted? This is exactly why.

If you look at the original language, the first and second times Jesus asked Peter if he loved Him, He used the word *agape*. He asked Peter, "Do you sacrificially love Me without conditions? However, when Peter responded with, "Yes, Lord, You know that I love You," he didn't use the word *agape*. He used

---

15   *Romans 8:32*

the word *phileo*, which means brotherly love. Jesus twice asked Peter if he shared the same love Jesus had for him. But, when Jesus put Himself out there, He got friend-zoned by Peter! The third time Jesus asked Peter if he loved Him, He used the word *phileo*, which explains why it crushed Peter.

"Do you really just like Me, Peter?" What amazes me is that Jesus responded the same way, even though Peter didn't have the same level of commitment to Jesus that Jesus had to Peter. Jesus told him, "Feed my sheep." In so few words, He said to Peter, "I know that you're not quite there yet, but I'm still going to partner with you. There will be a time you will love Me the same way I love you and I'm okay with the process."

This revelation exploded in my heart. Even though I'm not where I want to be with God, He still invites me in. We don't have to have it all figured out; He is just glad we still choose to show up.

BROKENNESS IS A GREAT PLACE TO START

There was a time in college that was one of the most difficult seasons of my life. I had gone through a gut-wrenching break-up and was trying to figure out who I was. My world seemed in shambles.

Although I didn't know it at the time (I felt miserable), I can see in retrospect that—as far as God was concerned—I was actually in a good place. As someone who consistently put relationships ahead of just about anything else, I had finally gotten to a spot where God was asking me to step up to the plate, so to speak, and I was actually listening.

One of my favorite verses in the Bible says, "Guard your heart above all else, for it determines the course of your life."[16] I think the reason it had been so challenging to come out of that particular relationship was I had allowed myself to become extremely enmeshed with the other person and had not taken the proper precautions in "protecting my heart" (or hers, for that matter). Now I felt God was leading me into a season of refraining from dating—a concentrated season of protecting my heart. I knew I needed to allow God to be first in my life, not myself and certainly not anyone else.

In the four years that followed, I may have gone on three dates. I was completely fixed on my career and my ministry with Young Life. It was during that season of "dating God" that He and I worked on me. The objective was that when He did bring me a spouse, I would have the character to sustain the blessing and the practice of being a source of love, instead of just reflecting it like a mirror. I knew I needed to become well practiced in turning to God with my problems rather than turning to a human being who was never designed to sit in the place of God. That's idolatry! And, although it was painful and lonely at times and I was certainly the most misunderstood guy in the Seahawks locker room, I wouldn't trade that season of my life for anything.

---

16   *Proverbs 4:23, NLT*

HERE COMES RACHEL

I remember putting on a podcast of a favorite pastor who was teaching about praying for God to bring you your spouse. I thought in my heart, *Okay, God, I finally get it, what You meant when You said it's not good for man to be alone.* I had great friends, a satisfying career, and a great purpose much deeper than playing professional football, but I still had a longing for companionship.

As I listened to this teaching, I heard the pastor begin to talk about Genesis 29, which is the story of how a man named Jacob met a woman named Rachel. (It's a cool story; if you've never read it, I encourage you to go check it out.) As I read through the story on my own, I began to sense that God was trying to show me something in it.

The pastor went on to talk about how he had written out a list of qualities he hoped for in a spouse. (Kind of the whole idea that if you don't know what you're aiming at, you will miss every time.) I took this teaching to heart and, in March of 2012, spent some valuable alone time with God. I pulled out my journal and began scribbling down things that my own heart longed for in a wife: that she would have to love God as much as me, that she would love me as much as I would love her, and that she would be kind and tender towards people. The first ten things I wrote had to do with her character and who I hoped she would be as a person. (The last thing I wanted was a pretty girl with an ugly soul. As Proverbs 11:22 says, "A beautiful woman who lacks discretion is like a gold ring in a pig's snout!" NLT)

That wasn't my whole list, though. The last four things may have been a little more carnal: that she would be tall, athletic, funny, and brunette. (Hey, the Bible also says, "Take delight in the Lord and he will give you your heart's desires," right?)[17] My friend Chris used to say, "Just look for Jesus in a bikini." It's a hilariously gross word picture but the point is powerful. I put the list away and promptly forgot about it.

Six months later, I was hosting a Young Life meeting when a beautiful woman named Matti came walking into my house—someone I had never seen before. She stopped me in my tracks. The whole planning meeting was an absolute waste of time for me. All I could do was watch this stunning woman and see how she interacted with everyone around her. She was magnetic.

I walked upstairs to get a breath of fresh air and the wife of our Young Life Area Director followed me. She came up to me and with a big smile on her face said, "You two are totally gonna date."

NO, was it that obvious? Did I just absolutely reek of desperation for this girl I barely knew? Quick! Clint, lock it up! Get things back in control. You're in a season of not dating remember? Yep, Got it. I smiled and said, "Yeah, we will see."

---

17   *Psalm 37:4, NLT*

I thought about that girl for months after that. The following February, our group was getting ready to go on a Young Life weekend trip down to a camp in Oregon called Breakaway. The Thursday before we were supposed to leave, I sat down to read my Bible. I had a reading plan that I hadn't done a great job following—it was the first time I had opened up my Bible in about two weeks.

Before I sat down, I thought back to the girl I had met at the Young Life planning meeting. I wondered if I was going to see her at this retreat. She was on the forefront of my mind as I flipped open my Bible to the assigned chapter of the day. About midway through reading it, I had a strange *deja vu* sensation come over me. *Have I been here before? This feels so familiar.* The feeling was overwhelming. I glanced up at the top of the page and it read, "Genesis 29."

I knew I had written something about this chapter before. Then, I remembered the list! I ran upstairs to grab my other journal. As I skimmed the entries of things I felt God had spoken to me, I finally stumbled upon that list of 14 things I had asked God for in a spouse almost a year earlier. There were things I had written down about how I would meet her, such as how it would be through some type of ministry event. That it would be at a time when I wasn't looking for her. That it would come out of the blue. That I wouldn't have to go out looking for her, but God would bring her to me. As I read through this list, a chill went up my spine and sudden tears ran down my face. *Was she the one?*

That weekend was incredible. We saw God move in a powerful way—so many kids encountered Jesus. I also got to hang out with this really pretty girl, even though I had to try exceptionally hard to not geek out and propose or something. (I'd had a word from God, for cryin' out loud!) There was no doubt some strong chemistry there. I think everyone in the room saw the sparks between us.

When we got home, I reached out to her and asked her out on a date. She said yes and I started naming the kids. We had one of those marathon dates—the kind that goes so well that you're not exactly sure when to stop it. We walked around Green Lake in Seattle with a cup of coffee for about three hours. It was perfect.

We had a few more dates and all of a sudden, I wasn't getting texts back. I thought, *What's the deal? Was it something I said? How will we ever get started on little Billy Gardenhoser Gresham?* That's when she sat me down and we had the "talk."

"Hey, you're a great guy and all, but I'm seeing someone and I need to see if this is going to work out." Knife to the heart! (In the back of my mind, all I was thinking was, *God, You said she was the one!)*

Cool as a cucumber (I still don't know what that means), I responded with, "Hey, you're an amazing girl and you are certainly the type of woman I would want to marry. I don't know if you would ever want to end up with me but I want you to know that I'll pray for you and ask God to bring the right man into your life." (Drop the mic.)

She smiled and thanked me for buying her a Sprite and we went our own directions. Even though I was hoping she would be so moved by my grand gesture of putting her first, I really did mean it that I would pray for her. So for the next month, every night at 9:00 pm I would walk into my basement, set a timer for 20 minutes, and pray for her. Not that she would marry me (that's twisted). I prayed she would encounter Jesus, that He would bless her life, and that she would end up with the man God had for her. I felt pretty sure I was the one for her but that was never my prayer. I really cared about this woman and just wanted to see God move in her life.

After five months of not communicating, I reached out to her and invited her to a housewarming party at my place. I had been so up and down, warring with God about whether this woman would be my spouse. I felt so confident that He had spoken to me, but had decided to hold it with an open hand. There would be lots of people at the house and this would be a great way to be around each other in a group setting. No agenda, just community in its purest form.

I finally realized she was *really* into me when I noticed her circling like a cat on the prowl when other girls would talk to me. When one particular girl walked away, Matti was practically pinned to my hip the rest of the night.

God took me through the wringer to finally end up with the woman He had chosen especially for me. While the season of being with Him was painful, it had to happen. Had I not learned how to depend on God for my needs, I would have codependently aligned myself with Matti. Had I not submitted myself to God's process of refinement, I don't believe we would have ended up together.   Good things tend to come to us more often when we choose to do life God's way. Matti and I ended up dating for a year, getting engaged, and getting married. It was perfect.

When we decide to do things God's way, we can rely on God's blessing. Don't ask God to bless what you're doing; do what God is blessing. It means taking time to be alone with Him to get His thoughts on your love life. You will never regret it.

THEN IT'S SETTLED

March 29, 2015 was the day I married Matti. About six weeks before that, I had begun a blended reading program on my Bible app that pulls a random chapter of Scripture each day for you to go over. When I woke up on our wedding day, I looked down at my phone and saw the passage of Scripture for that day was Genesis 29. That was the story of Jacob and Rachel that had been so impactful to me, and had started me on the path of praying for my future wife. *How on Earth does that happen?!* I was in complete awe.

And about those final four qualities I asked God for in a wife: tall, athletic, brunette, and funny? My wife Matti is six feet tall, played volleyball in college, has brown hair, and her dream is to be on *Saturday Night Live*. A relationship done God's way is an amazingly delicious and satisfying experience, like pizza for your soul. *Selah*.

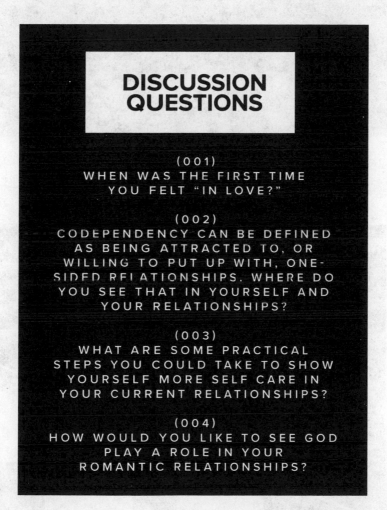

DISCUSSION QUESTIONS

(001)
WHEN WAS THE FIRST TIME YOU FELT "IN LOVE?"

(002)
CODEPENDENCY CAN BE DEFINED AS BEING ATTRACTED TO, OR WILLING TO PUT UP WITH, ONE-SIDED RELATIONSHIPS. WHERE DO YOU SEE THAT IN YOURSELF AND YOUR RELATIONSHIPS?

(003)
WHAT ARE SOME PRACTICAL STEPS YOU COULD TAKE TO SHOW YOURSELF MORE SELF CARE IN YOUR CURRENT RELATIONSHIPS?

(004)
HOW WOULD YOU LIKE TO SEE GOD PLAY A ROLE IN YOUR ROMANTIC RELATIONSHIPS?

LOVE
THE
PROCESS

The Denali Mountain Range gripped the Alaskan sky like the hand of God, its immovable beauty stealing the air from my lungs as I shot across the lake at 65 mph. The Sea-Doos a friend had loaned to Steve Hauschka (then kicker for the Seahawks) and me couldn't have come at a better time. But as we raced across the lake against this backdrop of God's creative beauty, my mind warred against me as if it still couldn't decide whose side it was on.

It was our third day in Alaska. Up until this point, Steve and I had caught almost 200 pounds of fish, had dinner with some of the most influential people in Alaska, and orchestrated a sports camp with dozens of special needs kids. Being an ambassador for the Seattle Seahawks was proving to be an absolute blast. (There are booster clubs all across the Northwest, so to interact with fans, the team will send players to engage with the community.) But as Steve and I walked up for a quick romp across the crystal clear lake, I heard the news there was going to be more than one snapper in training camp that season. My heart sank. My job was on the line.

Hearing bad news is never fun. Visions of defeat were flashing across the screen of my mind. I was tired of having to go out and defend my territory. One on one competition is uncomfortable, as you both know only one of you will make it out. It can bring out the worst in people. What made things even more complicated was that I had just began processing an idea for a video project investigating the ambition of excellence on and off the field.

I always viewed my time as a professional football player as an opportunity to influence people with the things in life that really matter. I'd seen so many high achievers over the years, in so many industries, who were great on paper but their home life was falling apart. I wanted to discover why some guys on the team seemed to not only excel on the field but also why they seemed to be so well adjusted. I called the project "The Making of a Champion."

The idea behind the video was to interview coaches and players from the Seahawks and talk to them about what really mattered in life. It was going to cost me about $25,000 and three months of work to make it happen—not an easy idea. And now my job was on the line in the midst of it. Tension was high, to say the least.

"What if he beats me out? I'm getting ready to produce a film saying I'm a part of the team. How foolish am I going to look when I pour my heart into something I felt God told me to do and it doesn't work out?" I empathized with how Noah

must have felt when God told him to build a boat. For years he built, most likely mocked by everyone, until the day the rain started.

THE PROCESS

When God makes a promise, it always seems to be connected to a toilsome process, which always seems to gives a strong impression that what God said isn't going to actually happen. Besides Noah, think of Moses leading slaves into the Promised Land, Joseph sitting in prison, or Jesus hanging on a cross. God's promises are oftentimes fulfilled only when we accept the processes that accompany them.

God seems to have this amazing way of turning our tests into testimonies. That's why choosing to focus on the process, which is the daily obedience of what He's called us to do, increases our chances of actually receiving the promise and of becoming the person we have always hoped to be.

TRUE GRIT

Do you know the story of Abraham? God made a lot of amazing promises to him: that He was going to prosper him, give him a son, make his name great, make him the father of many nations, and give his people their own country.[18] Wow!

---

18   See Genesis 12

When God first told Abraham all these things, Abraham thought it was outrageous. In fact, his wife laughed right out loud because it all seemed so unbelievable. Abraham and Sarah couldn't wrap their minds around the idea that God was going to give them a son when he was 75 and she was barren. Who wouldn't have thought that was crazy?

Waiting patiently has never been mankind's strongest character trait. We seem to have it ingrained in our biology to find the shortest route to an outcome in order to preserve the most amount of energy. The path of least resistance isn't just sought by the lazy; we all want things to be easy. The important thing is how much we allow our natural preference for comfort to influence our lives.

There was a coach who would shout during every Seahawks game while we were stretching, "Don't let the body control the mind; make the mind control the body!" I was always so intrigued by that idea. Our human brains are incredibly powerful organs that can unfortunately cause us trouble while trying to preserve our lives. The brain can promise the shortest path between two points but will often sacrifice God's process in favor of its process.

But back to Abraham: for 25 years, he waited to have his son. God made it perfectly clear to him the child was going to come through his wife, Sarah. But, like most humans, Abraham was impatient. We have a tendency to want to make things happen when we don't see a way, don't we? So when Sarah, Abraham's wife, approached him with the idea of having him father a child through her servant girl, Hagar, he agreed to it. I'm not sure why he didn't realize this was sidestepping God's plan. But this man, who thousands of years later God would refer to as the "father of faith," decided it was a good idea to get another woman pregnant as a shortcut to seeing the promise of God fulfilled. Abraham essentially made himself the answer to his own prayer.

Abraham's attempt to skip God's process by having a child through Hagar resulted in an additional 15 years of waiting. On top of that, it complicated things with what these days we might call "baby mama drama." Once Sarah saw Hagar was pregnant, the Bible says, "she despised her."[19]

I guarantee that, when we try to skip God's process and choose our plan over His, the end result will be a decay of some type. Whether it be in relationships, confidence, or hope, being the answer to your own prayer will not satisfy you and won't accomplish God's purposes either. God's promises require obedience and grit on our part.

We once had a speaker come and talk to the Seahawks, an expert on this topic. Angela Duckworth, author of the bestselling book *Grit*, told us that, basically, "grit" is passion and perseverance. It's the belief that setbacks do not easily sway you. It's a dogged inner resoluteness that seems to increase with each

19   *Genesis 16:4*

attack. It's also the number one predictor of success. It's the trait all of us want more of but most of us don't know how to actually develop.

As I sat in my chair with 100 other players and coaches, one thing that made a lot of sense to me was her comment, "There is zero connection between talent and grittiness." I think each of us can think of a least one person in our lives who had all the talent in the world but none of the drive to nurture that talent. Grit seems to be a talent in it of itself separate from any measurable success skills.

As Duckworth began to wrap up her presentation, she commented on how "we are still trying to understand how to increase grit in people." I got the sense that much of her research pointed to this idea that you either have it or you don't. I found myself disappointed. If you either have it or you don't, what are we doing here? If it's the most important trait in determining success, how can we grow it? She went on to say, "While we aren't exactly sure how to increase it, one indicator seems to lie in the idea of a process-based focus over an outcome-based focus." *Be patient. Embrace the process. I get it.*

Duckworth alluded to work done by Dr. Carol Dweck who has been a pioneer in exploring the power of a growth mindset over a fixed mindset. Dweck spoke of a high school in Chicago where students had to pass 84 units to graduate. If they didn't get those 84 units, they received the grade "Not yet" as opposed to the standard "Fail."

How amazing is that? If you get the grade "Fail," that's a difficult label to shake off. But getting the grade "Not yet" sets you up for growth in the future. You're on a learning curve that doesn't assassinate your sense of worth. "Not yet" provides a path to a future full of promise.

For children who have learned to have a growth or "process-based" mindset as opposed to a fixed mindset, a negative outcome doesn't blow them out of the water. Trying something new doesn't become a terrifying possibility of feeling stupid if they fail. Dweck went on to speak of some of the most notoriously underachieving schools in the country that, when they adopted this style of teaching, soared to the top. Quite simply, a positive growth mindset is the key to grit.

GRIT AND FOOTBALL

For six years, I sat five feet away from one of the greatest coaches in history. I can say from experience there is nobody better than Pete Carroll when it comes to creating culture. He might be the most disciplined man I have ever met when it comes to using his words like a surgeon's knife to assess and remedy any problem.

Coach Carroll never said a single thing about winning a Super Bowl, or even winning games for that matter. Practically every day he said the exact same thing over and over and over. When our team didn't believe we had what it took, he told us otherwise, convincing each and every one of us we were the best in the world at what we did.

When the Seahawks started off 2-4 at the beginning of the 2015 season, his message was no different. There wasn't a shred of anxiety in his voice. Every day he would talk about focusing on things we could control. Everywhere we looked, we saw reminders of where our focus should be. On the back of shirts, posters, and playbooks, we would see our four objectives, "Great effort, great enthusiasm, great toughness, and playing smart." He would rattle off the three rules of the team, which were "to protect the team, no whining/no complaining/no excuses, and to be early." It was like drinking from a performance fire hose.

None of these things had anything to do with anyone we were playing against. None of them had anything to do with an outcome. The focus was always on things that were in our control. It never mattered who we were playing. It didn't matter if it was a Super Bowl or a scrimmage; we treated everything the same. In fact, I recorded both speeches Coach Carroll gave to us the nights before Super Bowl 48 and 49 and both of them were practically the same ones he gave us the nights before many of our preseason games.

The thing about chasing an outcome—like a Super Bowl win, a particular answer to prayer, or a goal of any kind—is that, once you get it, oftentimes you can lose your hunger. It's the reason so many first round draft picks are a bust and the same reason most teams can't repeat Super Bowl appearances.

Since 1999, only two teams have gone to back-to-back Super Bowls: the Patriots and the Seahawks. The reason I went to two Super Bowls instead of one is because winning the Super Bowl was never the goal of the Seattle Seahawks. Our goal was to go out every day and make practice great. The process was the focus.

We were exhorted to love the things that get you to the big game—the things we had control over like our effort, enthusiasm, and positivity. By focusing on the process, the big moments always took care of themselves. This allowed us as a unit to have a growth mindset, which saw setbacks as opportunities for learning as opposed to reminders of failure. It's the reason the Seahawks won almost 90% of their games that were broadcast on prime time television. We rose to the occasion because we fell in love with the things that got us to that occasion.

WHAT'S YOUR GRIT QUOTIENT?

How do you handle difficult situations? A growth mindset says, "I love a challenge." A fixed mindset, on the other hand, sees adversity as catastrophic.

When you read the story of Jesus calling Peter out of the boat to walk on water, do you wonder why he was the only disciple to try something that had never been done before? Why was Peter always the first one to speak up, even when it was something dumb? Why did Peter not crumble in shame when Jesus called him "Satan"? Peter was a rock. Even Jesus called him that. He was a gritty guy who wasn't afraid to take chances, fail, or look dumb.

While Matti and I were first getting to know one another, we had a time for all of the Young Life leaders serving our area to get together and pray for each other. When it came time to pray for Matti, I had this picture pop into my mind of a butterfly coming out of its cocoon. I told her that if the butterfly didn't fight its way through the cocoon, it would lack the strength it needed to survive. If someone were to come along and pluck that butterfly out of its cocoon as a favor so it wouldn't have to fight, it would actually kill the butterfly. As I shared this with Matti, she began to cry. It resonated deeply with her. I think it's a truth that resonates with all of us. Pain is uncomfortable, especially if you have been indoctrinated to believe that painful situations are a direct attack on your worth and that they will expose your weakness as opposed to growing your strength.

TRUST THE PROCESS

I struggled in school most of my life. School felt like a persistent evaluation of worth; grades were character assessments. I felt stupid. I was diagnosed with ADHD, which meant my teachers hated me (at least that's what it felt like). It's probably why I always gravitated towards sports. The athletic field was a sacred place where I felt alive. It was where I got love. I learned quickly to dislike the teachers whom I always seemed to disappoint, but I tried hard for coaches who dangled the carrot of affirmation in front of me. I was praised for performance on the field, which fueled my drive but also cemented within me an outcome-based focus and a fixed mindset.

Financial accounting was by far the toughest class I remember taking. I had never worked so hard for a C in my life. I was proud of that C! I remember being on the phone with my dad and him telling me he was proud of how hard I had worked (praising effort). He talked about how hard that class was for him, too (empathy). When my dad used those two methods with me, I felt absolutely free of shame for not getting a better grade and free in knowing my effort was not in vain. Now, when I look back on that moment of getting a middling grade, I don't feel the slightest bit of humiliation. My dad's word's killed that humiliation years ago.

So many of us look back on disappointments in life with such overwhelming sadness, wishing things could be different. But when we apply a mindset that views setbacks, disappointments, or regrets as tools, it gives us the freedom to become whole. It takes our regrets and turns them into positives.

When I got into the NFL and began to learn more about focusing on the process, I began to see how ridiculously challenging it is to motivate people to think and work from a growth mindset in a culture that focuses on and rewards outcomes.

Score lots of touchdowns? Make lots of money? Make lots of money is supposed to be a statement, not a question. Snap a foot- ball through your legs perfectly every time? You can remain in our family.

In retrospect, I can see that so many of the coaches I have had throughout my life always seemed to be so wound up. Proba- bly it was because they felt their outcomes were being eval- uated, too. For any of us, there is real performance pressure in our careers. But by fixing our hearts to those outcomes, we can lose ourselves along the way. This is likely why so many coaches I had would use shame and humiliation to motivate players. When they find themselves scared for their job, they birth that same fear in others, making the environment around them just as miserable and unsustainable as their own.

When fear takes over, clear thinking goes out the window. We replicate our fear in other people, trying to motivate them. We carve them up with shame and humiliation because we don't have the grit to be able to see people for who they are "be- coming." Instead, we fixate on who they currently appear to be.

I have fought against a fixed mindset my entire life. I still ha- ven't arrived, but I know I'm growing in the discipline of fo- cusing on the process of who I am "becoming," rather than obsessing about the idealized person I hope to be someday.

When the Seahawks cut me, I felt like such a failure. The par- ticular moment of hearing the general manager say, "We found

"SPIRITUAL GRIT IS NOTHING MORE THAN UNWAVERING FAITH."

#BECOMINGBOOK

someone else," cut me deeply. Thoughts of defeat clouded my heart. After being released, I kept hearing rumblings that the team was considering bringing me back. One coach told me he wasn't sure what was going to happen and to stay ready. I had high hopes for coming back to the team. I would watch Seahawks games and hear the announcers say, "The number one thing the Seahawks need to do is to bring back Clint Gresham."

But after months of career purgatory, Matti and I decided the bravest thing for us to do was to move on and head back to Texas where both of our families were. We needed people who loved us unconditionally. Being in Seattle after being cut felt like driving past your ex's house every day. Everyone in town just adores her, and she seems to be doing so great without you. I laugh about it now but, at the time, it was painful.

Back in Texas, I was sitting at dinner one night hashing over the feelings of defeat with my mom. I had this recurring thought that, if I were just a little stronger, tried just a little harder, did just a little more, I would still be there. If I just had more grit, I'd be on the team.

She looked at me warmly and said, "Clint, you are already gritty. You played professional football for six years, twice the average. The Seahawks brought in competition every single season and you beat those guys out every time. You played in two Super Bowls. Honey, you already are a strong person."

Her words soothed me, like cold aloe vera on a bad sunburn. It caused a massive shift in my mindset. I began to feel lighter. The deep feelings of failure and regret began to fade. I quit seeing myself as a failure and started seeing myself as a person who was "becoming" something. I quit obsessing over the outcome of being cut and began seeing the entire thing as a beautiful process God was taking me through—establishing grit in me that I otherwise would never have.

SPIRITUAL GRIT

The power of grit is nothing new. King Solomon was right when he said, "There is nothing new under the sun."[20] Things are simply packaged in new and different ways and marketed as the buzz word of the day. If grit really is the number one indicator of success, is it possible something so timeless and powerful would be mentioned in the number one selling book of all time? What does the Bible have to say about this concept?

When you look at all the major players in the Bible, they always exhibited "grit." Think of Noah building an ark, Abraham waiting for Isaac, Jacob serving a devious uncle, Joseph sitting in prison, Moses leading people out of slavery, Rahab hiding the spies, David being anointed king way before he was actually appointed, Jesus hanging on a cross, and unwed Mary carrying a baby in a culture that stoned women for committing adultery. It seems the number one indicator of "spiritual

---

20   *Ecclesiastes 1:9, NKJV*

success" (people understanding and receiving God's promises) was also grit. Each person had a particular promise from God he or she was contending for and, while they all may have faltered with doubt at times, they stayed fixed on doing what God said to do. The end result? They received the promise.

As Jesus hung on the cross, He was aware He had the ability to skip the process and call down legions of angels to His rescue. What He chose to do was remain in the more difficult right place instead of the easier wrong place. Had Jesus skipped the process, we would all be in trouble! The Bible says it was for "the joy set before him that he endured the cross."[21] The promise God made to Him was what gave Him the strength to fight through the immediate pain for the long-term payoff.

The type of grit God is trying to establish in us isn't about a personality type or character trait. It's founded in God's strength, not ours, which means, as we grow in our revelation of His strength, grit grows in us. I think much of the research regarding grit is wonderful and has helped so many people, but grit founded apart from steadfastness in God's promises is practical atheism. It can lead to a mindset of not needing God even though we may give Him credit. On top of that, we can fall into the victim mindset I fell into when I first heard the researcher allude to the idea of either having it or not.

The grit God wants us to walk in must be fastened to His promises. In other words, spiritual grit is nothing more than

---

21   *Hebrews 12:2, NKJV*

unwavering faith: ". . . the substance of things hoped for, the evidence of things not seen."[22] It is the dogged, inner resoluteness of trusting God is going to do what He said He would in your life.

LIFE SAYS "THIS"; GOD SAYS "THAT"

God has always made a habit of calling things that aren't real as if they are.[23] I guess when you are the One who made everything, you can do stuff like that. It isn't a lie; it's just a higher reality. God gets what He speaks. He told Abram, "You're now Abraham." He told Jacob, "You're now Israel." He tells sinners, "You're now righteous." But when our entire understanding continues to point to our past, it can be difficult to adopt the way God views things.

When God was bringing the Israelites out of slavery and into the Promised Land, they all wanted to go back to where things were familiar, which was in slavery. He took His people out of Egypt but He couldn't get Egypt out of them.

When all you see are your shortcomings and faults, God sees you as righteous, pure, holy, and set apart. You see, God knew what He was getting into when He brought you into His family. When you accept what Jesus did on the cross for you, you are not a nasty old sinner. He calls you a saint.[24] But if you continue to think contrary to God's thoughts, you will always struggle because "as a man thinks in his heart, so is he."[25]

---

22 *Hebrews 11:1, NKJV; 23 Romans 4:17*
24 *2 Corinthians 5:17, 21; 25 Proverbs 23:7*

Many of us are clinging to the cross not with faith in Christ's finished work but in an attempt to die for our own sins, self righteously carrying around shame and discouragement. Our sins, shame, and discouragement were taken care of when we made Jesus Lord of our lives. It's time to begin to see yourself as God sees you, not what your situation, feelings, or experiences tell you to see. In 2 Corinthians 5:19, we find out, "God was reconciling the world to himself in Christ, not counting people's sins against them. And he has committed to us the message of reconciliation" (NIV). What that tells you is that God doesn't hold your sin against you, because He has already held it against Jesus on your behalf. That's why to walk around with shame or condemnation is so unnecessary.

He carried your sin so you don't have to anymore. That means you can fall in love with the person you are becoming because, in God's eyes, you have already been perfected. That was sealed when you came into His Kingdom. When you confess something as sin to God the first time, He forgives you; when you confess the same thing again because you're beating yourself up about it, He doesn't know what you are talking about. You are free from your past!

REDEFINE SUCCESS

What does God see when He sees you? He sees you completely differently from how you see yourself. If He is God, and knows more than us; maybe we should look at ourselves the way He looks at us! If you believed about yourself what God believes about you, you would be unstoppable in every single area of your life. The only thing capable of stopping you would be the fixed mindset, which says setbacks are definers of worth, not learning opportunities.

I used to have a bunch of shame when people would say, "You are who you are when no one is looking." Or, "During tough times, the real you comes out." Unfortunately, both of those statements just end up being another way people assign identity based on performance, instead of how God assigns identity based on His grace.

It seems to be ingrained in everyone to want to look perfect to the people around us. All of us want to be perceived as competent and strong. Plus, religion can give us so much ammo to judge whether someone is "good" or not, instead of seeing people like God sees them. The truth is though, we're all less than perfect when "no one's looking." When we are alone, we can be the normal, fallible, imperfect humans that we are, instead of the airbrushed versions of ourselves we think society expects of us.

In addition, to say that the real you is who you are during your worst moments is a contradiction to how God sees you. The real you is the one Jesus thought was worth dying for. You are not restricted to your worst moment. Just because you gave into a temptation in an attempt to soothe sadness in your life doesn't mean you're now branded forever by your shortcomings. (Come on now, is that really how we should be judging who people are?)

The reality is that people only change in the presence of unconditional love; they will never change when we assign them a label of "x" because they struggle with a particular flaw. "WWJD" (What Would Jesus Do?) is aspirational, slogan; we will never hit it perfectly. We are all trying to be like Jesus. But if you don't learn to like yourself while you are "becoming" you will only find yourself bound with shame and stay stuck in the same struggle forever.

When people try and label you with your struggle, remember you are who God says you are, NOT WHO PEOPLE SAY YOU ARE.

It doesn't mean things are going to be easy. They will not be easy. We are in the process of "becoming" like Jesus. We aren't like Him yet; as long as we are on this side of Heaven, we will have struggles. You are set free from the expectation that you should have already arrived. Your ups and downs are merely part of the story God is telling through your life.

Throughout our entire lives we are programmed to focus on outcomes—grades, behavior, church, sports. I mean, honestly look back at your childhood and see if there was any praise that happened that wasn't connected with you accomplishing

"GOD DOESN'T SEE YOU THROUGH THE LENS OF FAILURE YOU DO."

#BECOMINGBOOK

something. I think the majority of us would say that was the norm. But long term, it doesn't work.

Employers today find themselves frustrated because their employees can't seem to make it through a day without needing some type of validation or praise. We've become addicted to the need for notoriety, desperate for the created to tell us "well done" instead of leaning into our Creator for our sense of worth. It's our responsibility to look to a Father in Heaven and find out what He has to say about us.

God flat out says, "My thoughts are not your thoughts."[26] Our thoughts are thoughts of failure; His are thoughts to give us a future and a hope.[27] Look at the thoughts God had for Abraham, the man who compromised by sleeping with a woman who wasn't his wife to make God's promise happen in his own timing, "He did not waver at the promise of God through unbelief, but was strengthened in faith giving Glory to God, and being fully convinced that what he had promised he was also able to perform and therefore it was accounted to him for righteousness."[28]

Now, hold on a second. How could that be true? I mean, Abraham thought his wife's plan of having a child through a different woman was a good idea. And, he went through with it! But when God made record of it in the book of Romans, He spoke of Abraham as this unwavering rock of faith who was absolutely persuaded that God was going to do what He said He would do. Abraham compromised, yet God called him the

---

26   *Isaiah 5:8, NKJV*
27   *Jeremiah 29:11, NKJV*
28   *Romans 4:20-22 NKJV*

father of faith even though he did something worthy of being fired for by most churches.

How audacious for God to consider someone who failed as somone who was worthy of praise! How could God call David "a man after God's own heart," when he committed murder and adultery and lied about it for months? Maybe God doesn't see you through the lens of failure you do. Maybe He sees you as a person of grit, the way He saw Abraham. If God sees you as someone with grit, maybe you should see yourself that way, too!

Our minds have a nasty habit of supplying us with evidence that we don't measure up or aren't doing enough. Our bent towards self disqualification is in desperate need of reprogramming. It's our responsibility to get into God's Word and ingest His promises in our hearts and minds. By doing so, we elevate our spiritual grit. Growing your grit comes from changing your perspective and being faithful to do the things God tells you to do. It's a muscle that must be exercised by being put into increasingly challenging situations.

GRIT GROWTH

The Chinese bamboo is a fascinating plant. For the first four years of its life, you don't see much above ground. In our instant gratification culture, the plant would be deemed a failure. But what we don't see is that the plant is in the process of creating a massive root system that will end up being the most important element to its survival for the rest of its life. What happens in the fifth year of its life cycle is incredible. The plant that seemed to produce no measurable success suddenly shoots up 80 feet in one year.

Most people call situations like this an overnight success. Those same people are the ones who want fifth year results without four years of prep. They forget the power of persistence and focusing on the process. They fail to realize that, without the first four years, the fifth year wouldn't be possible.

Spiritual grit and process-focused living mean sticking to your future, not just for the week or month, but for years, even when life has given you every reason to give up on it. Think of Joseph who dreamed he was going to be a ruler. But for years, he was stuck in prison for something he didn't do. Maybe you feel similarly. Remember that the promise God gave you for that business, ministry, or dream must be faithfully stewarded the same way in year one as it should be in year five.

When you see no fruit and everyone else is throwing in the towel, are you committed enough to the process that your effort and enthusiasm shine with the hope of God's promises? Don't stop being your best just because you're not yet where you want to be.

Before I left for Arizona with the Seahawks to play the Patriots in Super Bowl 49, I put a highlight reel of all my best snaps on my iPad to help me visualize how I wanted to perform during that game. I had two snaps in that game that were most likely un-noticed by everyone else, but they weren't up to my standard. When the outcome I wanted didn't happen, I went back to my highlight reel. It allowed me to put my failure behind me and to focus on my next opportunity. Where is your focus when opposition comes?

THE CHAMPION WAS MADE

It was after the second pre-season game of the 2013 season when my agent called me with the contract offer from the Seahawks. It was a great deal. This meant they were cutting the more athletic, taller, better looking (and, I thought, all around better) snapper and sticking with me for another few seasons. I was amazed and relieved.

I had poured so much time into our film, *The Making of a Champion*, trying to share with the world what it meant to us to be a champion in life. And God came through. The $25,000 video project I produced, concluding with leading people in prayer to receive Jesus at the 50-yard line in the Seahawks' home stadium, was worth it. My amazing team of volunteers and I passed out 28,000 copies of the film at the conclusion of one of the Seahawks games and, within a week, had over 100,000 views on YouTube.

That season, the Seahawks went on to destroy the Denver Broncos in Super Bowl 48 and became world champions. It was almost as if, in a prophetic sense, God honored our "Making of a Champion" project by actually giving us a championship.

I think back to those low moments of believing I should quit the project. I was spending money I didn't have to try and share Jesus with the world in a unique way. Had I quit on the process, who knows what would have happened? I can guarantee I would have had a massive amount of regret.

NO WEARINESS

God knows where He is taking you. If He were to give you a blessing before you were ready for it, it would be a curse. He knows what it takes to get you to where He wants you to be. More importantly, He knows what it takes to keep you there! Keeping fixed on trusting His process is the insurance policy for His promises.

I heard of a woman who gave birth to a child prematurely; the baby girl was under one pound. She spent almost a year in the hospital and had to have several surgeries. Thankfully, the baby ended up okay. The point is, though, that while giving birth to something too early may be easier because you don't have to carry it as long, it isn't God's best. The longer you must wait, the bigger the dream God is birthing in you and the healthier it will be when you let it come to full term.

When you find yourself frustrated that you haven't birthed your dream, fix your heart back on the process. An elephant is pregnant for two years; a rabbit is pregnant 31 days. Imagine a conversation between the two. The rabbit says, "You're not pregnant; see, I've given birth to hundreds of rabbits. It's been 18 months and you still haven't given birth."

The elephant responds, "Well, you see, I'm giving birth to something big, something special, something you don't see every day. That's why it's taking longer." If the elephant were to fall victim to the doubts proposed by the rabbit, it would lose out on the joy of the process.

People around you may be giving birth to dreams; be happy for them. When all you see are the outcomes of others' processes, put your focus back on where it needs to be, on your process—the promise God has made to you for your situation. Never forget, the reason it's taking a long time to see the evidence of your process is because, like the elephant, what you are carrying isn't ordinary. What you are going to birth is going to be bigger and more rewarding than something that happens immediately.

Whatever the outcome you are looking for, focus on the process. Be engaged in this very present moment of time. What do you sense God has called you to do? Pursuing it will establish "spiritual grit."

What can you do right now to help get yourself to where you know you are destined to be? Jesus said not to worry about tomorrow; doing that is just going to create anxiety, which will create more problems.[29]

Trusting the process is synonymous with trusting God's character. Do you believe He is who He said He was for you? Stay fixed in this present moment, leaning into His promises. He will never leave you. And He will make it happen in His timing.

---

29   *Matthew 6:34*

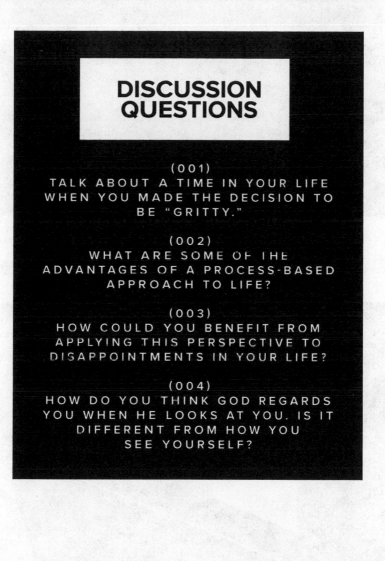

DISCUSSION QUESTIONS

(001)

TALK ABOUT A TIME IN YOUR LIFE
WHEN YOU MADE THE DECISION TO
BE "GRITTY."

(002)

WHAT ARE SOME OF THE
ADVANTAGES OF A PROCESS-BASED
APPROACH TO LIFE?

(003)

HOW COULD YOU BENEFIT FROM
APPLYING THIS PERSPECTIVE TO
DISAPPOINTMENTS IN YOUR LIFE?

(004)

HOW DO YOU THINK GOD REGARDS
YOU WHEN HE LOOKS AT YOU. IS IT
DIFFERENT FROM HOW YOU
SEE YOURSELF?

07

WORTH IT ALL

I know most people probably say this, but I seriously mean it when I say that my wedding day—the day I married Matti—was the best day of my life. My mentor Eric did an amazing job as our officiant, I ugly cried in front of everyone during the ceremony, and we all danced for hours. To top off an already perfect evening, we realized our wedding served as a point of connection and healing for people. That night, we saw family members who hadn't spoken in years crying happy tears and hugging each other. It was a remarkable thing to witness and be a part of. Understandably, it was a day I'd been anticipating for a long time.

Most of the people who came probably had no clue how much time and money went into planning the day. As much as the day was about us, it was also about exceptionally loving the people who came to our ceremony. The week leading up to the wedding, I spent more time hand writing notes and wrapping presents for groomsmen, bridesmaids, aunts, uncles, and grandparents than I spent with Matti! Both of us had decided early in our courtship that our marriage was going to be about serving others and bringing them into something beautiful rather than selfishly accumulating wealth, status, or joy for ourselves.

Months before, as we began brooding over our guest list, we were faced with the reality that there were people we cared about whom we weren't going to be able to invite to our wedding. The numbers were just getting too high. This meant the people we were going to invite had to be extremely involved in our lives. For me, that was gut wrenching. (I took a test one time identifying my strengths and I tested highest in the category "includer," which means I would rather get a paper cut on my eyeball than for someone to feel left out.)

As we finalized our guest list, I began reaching out to people to get addresses for the formal invitations. I was surprised to find that, even in the process of asking for an address, I felt terribly exposed. By inviting this person to the most important day of my life, I was clearly communicating how much that person meant to me! The time between the "ask" and the "response" was a chasm of discomfort, leaving me with an expanding pit in my stomach. The fear of rejection felt so heavy. When you ask people to attend the most important day of your life, you hope the regard they have for you equals the regard you have for them. And that's what I was nervous about.

There was one particular individual whom I held in very high esteem. He had been (and still is!) a huge influence on my life in many ways. When I asked him for his address, I didn't hear back from him for about four days. I felt so naked. I wished the whole time I could un-send the text. When I finally heard back from him, things got worse. "Oh shoot, sorry. I don't know it."

What?! You don't know your address? Really? Maybe he didn't really know it, but it felt like an excuse. I was humiliated and mad. I mean, if you don't want to come to my wedding, that is completely okay, don't come. Just say you can't make it. But your address may be worth learning if you want to drive home after work or get any mail.

The underlying message I perceived was this: *My inherent value is low in comparison to my peers. You need a certain amount of notoriety to be a part of this circle, and we don't cross-pollinate.* But really, how could I know exactly what he thought of me? Who knew what might really have been going on in his mind? I concluded rejection because I was already anticipating it. Our brains will always search for evidence of things we already believe. Putting ourselves in other people's heads, as if we can really know what they're thinking, is what I call risky business, and it rarely ends well.

MANY CALLED, FEW CHOSEN

Rejection is pretty much part of the human experience, no matter how old we are. What we need to recognize is that our value has very little to do with how other people regard us.

When we absorb the truth that we are made in His image, the colossal gap between a perfect God and broken humanity starts to shrink. It's not that we need Him any less; we gradually become more like Him! Do you want to know why you feel love? It's because God is love. Why you get jealous? He does, too. Why you feel rejected? It's the story of His existence.

In the Bible, in Matthew's account of Jesus' life, he relays a story Jesus told about what life with God is all about:

> *The kingdom of heaven is like a certain king who arranged a marriage for his son, and sent out his servants to call those who were invited to the wedding; and they were not willing to come. Again, he sent out other servants, saying, 'Tell those who are invited, "See, I have prepared my dinner; my oxen and fatted cattle are killed, and all things are ready. Come to the wedding.' But they made light of It and went their ways, one to his own farm, another to his business...But when the king heard about it, he was furious...Then he said to his servants, 'The wedding is ready, but those who were invited were not worthy. Therefore go into the highways, and as many as you find, invite to the wedding.' So those servants went out into the highways and gathered together all whom they found, both bad and good. And the wedding hall was filled with guests.*[30]

I get why God was frustrated at the people who came up with all kinds of excuses as to why they didn't think He was worth

---

30   *Matthew 22:2-10, NK*

their time. Because of their inaccurate assessment of His value, they missed out on something beautiful. They didn't see the value in Him and missed out on the relationship. He decided to go out and find people who would appreciate the sacrifice, not because God needed His ego stroked, but because sacrifice as monumental as His is worthy of regard. God has called everyone, but He chooses the people who choose Him.

We see the same thing in the Old Testament, where God had to deal with people who didn't hold Him in high regard. God dreamed of giving His people their own country—of taking them out of Egypt where they were slaves for 400 years and showering them with love. But on the road to Israel, they continued to reject Him and make excuses. The result was that an eleven-day "geographical" journey to their own country and out of slavery ended up taking 40 years!

The patience God continued to show His children during that season continues to amaze me. For 40 years, the people He created were rebellious, stubborn, ungrateful, and downright wicked. He gave them countless opportunities until He finally decided He couldn't trust those people to be good stewards of the land He wanted to give them. So He set a boundary. He told them anyone above 20 years old wouldn't make it in, but He would bring their children into the land He had promised to give them.

THE ONLY

WAY TO FIN

TO UNDERS

GOD SAYS

ASTING

O VALUE IS

TAND WHO

OU ARE.

God opened His heart up to humanity. He gave His creation the power to accept Him or reject Him. He gave them free will so they could choose to love Him or not. After all, love is only real if it is given a choice.

I realize God is perfect and this probably goes without saying, but I have always been impressed with how non-personally God took His creation rejecting Him. You didn't see Him having a pity party in Heaven with Jesus and the Holy Spirit, asking why the people wouldn't love Him. It wasn't some middle school codependent romance where He needed them to love Him. No, God was absolutely secure in who He was. Was He angry with them? Yes. Did it make Him question whether He was worthy of love? Not in the least!

LEARNING TO LOVE YOURSELF

The message I received when the guy didn't give me his address wasn't simply, *I don't value you,* but was, *You are not valuable.* A colossal difference! One says, "You're not important to me." The other says, "You're not important to anyone." I got over it. But it was a good heads up for me about what was really in my heart: the fear of rejection and the fear I was not valuable. Such a lie! Unfortunately, these days, there seem to be far too many people believing the same lie, causing all kinds of self hatred and brokenness.

Now hear me on this: it's absolutely fine this individual didn't want to come to my wedding. I get it. I'm not any different; there are certainly people in my own life I hold in higher regard than others. My brothers and sister mean more to me than the guy serving me food at a restaurant. Just because I value my family more than someone else doesn't negate someone else's inherent value. Just because this particular individual didn't feel compelled to come to my wedding doesn't mean I'm not valuable. That guy was not the problem; my reaction was the problem.

BEGGING TO BE NOTICED

We live in a society today aching for significance. Some of us are shattered over the slightest bit of rejection, unable to hear constructive criticism. We fall apart if someone we know unfriends or un-follows us on social media. The insecure man is constantly looking for an "atta boy" from a world disdainfully mumbling, "You're not quite enough." Self respect seems to be a moving target that indifferently nods approval when you perform and ignores you when you fail. But you can be assured: the world's fiat currency of praise is cheap, and you are more valuable than you realize.

God says, "I know the thoughts I think towards you . . . thoughts of peace and not evil, to give you a future and a hope."[31] But while God knew the things He thought about me, I didn't. At

---

31   *Jeremiah 29:11, NKJV*

least, not to the point of being completely free from the shackles of people pleasing. And, since I didn't have a revelation of what He thought about me, I was stuck with all the things (I thought) everyone else thought about me, which is exhausting to maintain.

If you have a hungry soul void of the truth of your God-given significance, constantly looking for approval, you will drift from person to person, making them your god and asking them to be something they were never created to be. You will be blown out of the water at their dismissal of you, because nothing is more traumatic than being a disappointment to your "god." You will be embittered, reactionary, passive, and most likely despised.

Is this any way to live? NO!

We have this nasty habit of holding up the opinion of powerful personalities as if they are God. Unkind people can make a rude comment to you, baiting you into insecurity, hoping they can get you to doubt your value. In so doing, these predatory individuals will be licking their chops at the freshly massacred offering made to their own diminishing sense of worth. Damaged people will go to great lengths for a shot at feeling strong. It's why you see girls fall for jerks and why nice guys get walked on. Those whose sense of power is derived from their ability to squelch other peoples' power don't know what real power is. The only lasting way to find value is to understand who God says you are.

Rarely do you see someone make it into adulthood without some type of esteem issues, either like the ones I just described or some variation. The ones who say they don't might swing to the other end of the spectrum—narcissism and arrogance. Our society is so complex and full of mixed messages that it can be near impossible to love yourself the way God expects you to. Even the very idea of loving yourself comes across as twisted and egotistical, especially to people who are self righteously religious. We regularly quote what Jesus said about loving your neighbor as yourself, but the measure of love we have for our own soul is the same measure we will use towards our neighbor!

So if you hate yourself, the formula falls apart. You will do nice things for people, but it will never be from a sincere place. When you don't get the desired reaction for your service, hatred will bubble up in your heart. But wait a minute! You did it because you loved them right? Wrong! You did it because you wanted to be loved. And thus the cycle of performance, approval-seeking, and resentment continues.

When I was in the NFL, I often struggled with my role on the team. To be honest, the pecking order doesn't get much lower than the long snapper. I was supposed to stay quiet, do my job, and be unnoticeable. There might have been a game or two where a fellow player asked me to bring him water. It seemed the unspoken rule for me was, "Only speak if spoken to."

Don't get me wrong; there were times when it was great. I led men's groups, Bible studies, and prayer meetings. I produced *The Making of a Champion,* which has had combined views around five million. But in my last couple of seasons, the game took a toll on me and my self worth.

From the top, we were always told that being yourself would be celebrated. But oftentimes, being yourself didn't bring the validation many of us were hungry for. So we would bend and allow ourselves to be molded into what people hoped we would be. I wish I knew then what I know now. Your need for significance must be met apart from anything external like your career, financial success, or even your relationships. Loving who you are is an inside job, and it's no one's responsibility except your own. When you respect yourself, you will earn respect from others.

You cannot love someone authentically if you do not love yourself, and you cannot love yourself properly until you see how much God loves you. If you don't let God show you why He thought you were worth dying for, your love for others will always be codependent and self serving. It won't be love at all. It will be a kind of lust: you scratch my back and I'll scratch yours. You provide my self worth and I'll provide yours. How very selfish and weird that is!

Reciprocal love is shallow love. God calls us to be full of His love, able to freely give it with no strings attached. We're to be

---

32   *Matthew 6:33, ISV*

like the sun, not the moon. We make the decision to love first, not just reflect what we get from others.

Jesus said, "But first be concerned about God's kingdom and his righteousness, and all of these things will be provided for you as well."[32] God's Kingdom is one of perfect love. By choosing to love whether or not we get love in return, God promises to meet the desires and needs of our hearts. When you begin to search out seeing the gold in others, soon people start seeing the gold in you. Don't worry about being interesting; be interested.

STAND UP FOR YOUR VALUE

There was a gym in town where quite a few of my friends were training, so I thought I'd give it a shot, too. I went in for an initial consultation and was shocked at how much it was going to cost. But I really didn't have time to shop around for other trainers, so I bit the bullet and went for it.

For the most part, the training was okay, but not really anything special. I really prefer training in a group rather than one-on-one. After about five weeks, I found out a group of my buddies were all training there together, so I decided to jump in with them. A guy in the group told me the price was about a third of what I was paying for a private session and I was getting to train with guys I consider brothers. It was a win-win.

When I talked to one of the coaches at the gym, the quote he gave me to train with the group was about twice the amount of what my buddy told me he was paying. I was confused. I began reaching out to other guys in the group and most of them were either paying half of what I was told or didn't even respond to my question. I later found out most of them weren't paying anything at all. My first thought was: *Clint, be humble. Don't be demanding. You represent Jesus, which means you need to be nice . . .*

I called up my mentor Eric and talked it out with him. Before I could even finish what I was saying about trying to be humble, he vehemently cut me off. He said, "You are not there to subsidize anyone else's workout! That isn't who you are. Don't let him treat you like that!" He was enraged. It shocked me at first. I really didn't see what he saw. But as he continued to explain his frustration at how poorly this guy was treating me in his attempt to take advantage, I got mad—really mad.

Where was this anger coming from? Why was I getting mad? Shouldn't I be a nice Christian boy who doesn't ask too much— eating vanilla ice cream once a month after volunteering at a retirement home, driving under the speed limit, and wearing pressed khaki pants to church four days a week? How else was I supposed to get people to know Jesus?

Perhaps I needed to re-define the phrase, "What would Jesus do?" Jesus was not (and is not) a wimp. So if you're trying to be like Him, don't you be one either. I think about when Jesus started flipping a bunch of tables in the temple when people were treating God's house with disrespect. Or when He called a bunch of religious people "children of Satan" when they tried to shut Him down. Yours truly desperately needed some clarity on "WWJD."

When I was about ten years old, I went to a place called "Joy Camp." It sounds weird, I know. Honestly, it was weird. The only thing I remember is getting chastised multiple times when I would use the word "hate." Saying that word was like dropping an F-Bomb. If someone were to say, "Man, I hate it when I don't get picked to play basketball," or, "I hate it when that older guy bullies me," a well-meaning counselor would gasp and say, "God doesn't hate, because He is love! If you are going to say that, you will say, 'I strongly dislike' instead of the word 'hate.'"

Now, besides the fact that what he said was completely unbiblical (because God hates things that interfere with love), it was just weird. I strongly disliked Joy Camp.

God is not passive, wimpy, or pitiful. Following Him does not mean dying to the whims of everyone around us. As a kid who grew up in church, I often heard sermons about dying to ourselves and turning the other cheek. These are grounded in biblical truth, but it does not mean that as believers we must be doormats to the world.

What the counselor said to me that day weakened my self respect, perpetuating the idea that everyone else's needs were much more important than mine. While there are truths to laying down your life and being generous, if your service is not coming from a full well of self acceptance, your tank will run dry quickly.

BECOMING COMFORTABLE WITH . . . ME

My phone conversation with Eric about the training gym was one of the first times in my life I felt permission to be angry. Something shifted in me that day. My self respect began to grow and I became more and more convinced that standing up for myself might be the most Christlike thing I had done in years. My worth was far above how this guy was treating me.

During my years spent playing professional football, I didn't see the value in myself God thought was worth dying for, so I never put boundaries in place to demonstrate to people how they should treat me. It wasn't until recently I realized that letting people get the best of me isn't humility. We are the whipping posts of nobody, and deserve to be treated with absolute respect. But I hate to break it to you: if you don't respect yourself first, nobody else will.

I fought this internal battle constantly while playing in the NFL. I was always on the alert—always trying to be better than I was the day before. I felt like I was always "competing" and, deep down, I desperately just wanted to be accepted by a big, powerful industry. I would morph into whom I thought people would like and say things out of character to get the reaction I was looking for. In retrospect, I can see why I became so troubled.

I came to the NFL insecure. I was in love with God, but I was not solid on what He thought of me. I would have spikes of courage, but then would drop to lows of defeat during which I would feel ashamed for my initial spike of courage. *I'm so stupid; I knew I shouldn't have said that. They probably think I'm so dumb. No wonder no one likes me!* I had a well-meaning older guy tell me one time, "If you want to influence your teammates for Christ, do your job on the football field well." The problem was, my role as the long snapper made me feel like either a snap was unnoticed (a good snap), or a terrible failure (bad snap). I understand what he was trying to say, but someone's salvation should not be dependent on my long snapping performance!

This would always create a barrage of accusing, demeaning, and self-deprecating thoughts. I placed on myself shame upon shame. I didn't believe how valuable I was. I refused to believe the vastness of Christ's love for me, just the way I was.

Loving and believing man's acceptance over God's is the most deadly drug in existence. It seeps in to every realm of your life, causing you to inflate when praised and melt when criticized. The truth is, nothing will make you hate yourself more than trying to win the approval of people who have no business assigning your worth.

WHAT'S YOUR VALUE WORTH TO YOU?

So what is value anyway? Quite simply, value is determined by how much someone is willing to pay for something. For example, the Mona Lisa is more valuable than my kindergarten portrait. It happens to be worth 780 million dollars; my picture, on the other hand, is only worth maybe a few hundred dollars to my mom. However, my friends, you must know that your Creator paid the ultimate price for you. Your Creator—our Abba Father—says you are priceless. I could never put enough words on this page to describe how valuable you are to Him.

I had a chance a few years ago to speak at one of the greatest places on the planet (in my opinion)—Malibu Club. (Malibu Club is a gorgeous waterfront property in British Columbia, Canada, owned by Young Life.) As I was preparing for my first talk to about 350 teenagers, I kept having these thoughts about value bubble up in my heart. You hear people say, "God loves you" all the time. In fact, it can get so repetitive, you probably start to underestimate or disregard the intensity of His love.

Before my talk, I started thinking about how much God the Father loves His Son Jesus. I mean, they have been together for all eternity! They created the world we live in together. They are unbelievably intertwined. Yet, when it came time for God to redeem mankind (us) and give us a way out of our mess, God bought an opportunity to have us. He paid for our redemption with the life of the most priceless thing in existence to Him: His beloved son. Take a moment to let that sink in. God sacrificed Jesus for you.

Any intelligent investor or financial advisor would tell you to never exchange something for something else of lesser value. If you are going to barter, you must get something of at least equal—preferably greater—value in exchange. If God the Father, who is unconditionally in love with His son Jesus, chose to exchange His Son for us, what does that say about His love for us?

The very idea of this seems scandalous. Could God really love us that much? The answer is a resounding yes. Your inability to truly and deeply love yourself stems from the lack of understanding of how much God really loves you, His child. Our capacity as humans to love others and ourselves is dependent on Him. We love because He first loved us. God is love.

When we do not fully comprehend, understand, or even believe the sheer vastness of His love for us, we are unable to function at optimum capacity. Until you allow yourself to believe how valuable you are to God, you will be your own worst enemy. You will learn to tolerate abusive relationships, you will treat your body poorly, you will hate what you see in the mirror—the list goes on.

You are a prized possession—an invaluable jewel worth far more than the Mona Lisa. When you believe this and walk in this truth, your love for yourself will be made evident through the fruit of your life. There is gold in you Jesus thought was worth dying for. It's time for you to see the same gold He sees. God looked down on humanity and thought the blood of Jesus was a fair price. That feels so overwhelmingly uncomfortable to even say because, so often, all we see are the ways we don't measure up. Remember, it was God's idea to spend Jesus to buy us. We didn't twist His arm about it.

We moan and groan over the wonderful price God paid for us, forgetting the fact that God thought it was a great deal! Most of the time when I hear people talk about how high the price was, the unsaid truth is, ". . . and I'm not worth that." When you don't believe you are worth it, you will always push away the good things God wants to give you. Jesus' payment to get you was not a rip off to God. God is a much better investor than Warren Buffet. And He definitely doesn't have buyer's remorse!

Accept His *agape* love. It will change the way you see yourself, and change the way you see others.

DISCUSSION QUESTIONS

(001)
WHY IS HEALTHY SELF-ESTEEM
SO IMPORTANT?

(002)
IS IT EASY OR DIFFICULT TO LOVE
YOURSELF? WHY?

(003)
WHY DO YOU THINK IT CAN FEEL SO
UNCOMFORTABLE WHEN SOMEONE
WANTS TO SHOW US REAL LOVE?

(004)
HOW HAVE YOU LIVED IN A WAY
THAT WOULD DEMONSTRATE YOU
BELIEVE PEOPLE ARE BIGGER
THAN GOD?

THE WORLD IS A VAMPIRE

There was a guy I played football with who was one of the best in the world at what he did. He worked hard and was respected by all (teammates and fans alike). If our general manager and head coach could have had a son, he would be their guy.

This guy has been through a lot in his life and doesn't let anyone get close to him easily (like most high achievers, I've found). He and I would have occasional moments of conversation during which he'd open up, but I could count them on one hand. Most of the time, his attitude toward me was a mix of aloofness and downright hostility—scare tactics to keep me from knowing him. I used to reassure myself, thinking, *Deep down, I know he cares about me.*

To be honest, now I question it, not because I don't think he liked me (although at times I suspected he despised me), but because I don't think he has ever allowed anyone in. No one. Closeness, for some, is weakness, especially in the dog-eat-dog world of the NFL.

One time he saw me reading a book called *Scary Close* by my friend Don. I told him what it was about and he mocked me, telling me I had "issues." Years ago, I would have been crushed by his statement. Now, those kinds of things don't bother me. The truth is, all of us have issues! In 2 Corinthians 12:9, Paul says, "But he said to me, 'My grace is sufficient for you, for my power is made perfect in weakness.' Therefore I will boast all the more gladly about my weaknesses, so that Christ's power may rest on me."

The only way to live a wholehearted, fulfilling, and abundant life is to boast in your weakness. Boasting in your weakness is simply telling someone you trust the one thing you don't want to tell anyone. It could be, "I looked at porn," or, "I stole money from someone," or, "I cheated on a test." By bringing your weakness out into the light of trusted community, you take its power away from it. Sin and weakness no longer fester when the weapons of vulnerability and connection are used against them.

When I sit back and think about my old teammate, I realize I was probably one of the most threatening people in the world to him. Why? Because I saw through his mask. I could see how he was hurting and that made him uncomfortable. So, despite my efforts to connect, I was always left feeling humiliated. His fear of intimacy isolated him from real, meaningful relationships.

The bottom line: it takes more courage for a man to allow himself to be vulnerable and form real, meaningful connections than to play a football game in front of a bunch of fans who will eventually forget his name. The person I respect the most in the world is not the All-Pro Athlete. It is the individual who chooses to put down the mask and be authentic with his or her scars.

OUR NEED FOR CONNECTION

Recently I stumbled upon an interesting study suggesting what a powerful need connection really is. The study put a bunch of rats in individual cages. In each of the cages, the rats were given two water bottles. One water bottle was filled with water and the other was filled with water mixed with cocaine. The researchers monitored the behavior of these rats and watched as they took a little sip of the regular water and then went back to the water with the cocaine in it. Eventually, the rats only drank the cocaine water. In time, all the rats in the experiment died of an overdose.

Looking at this study, you could determine a few things: first, cocaine is addictive (thank you, Captain Obvious). Secondly, given the choice, rats prefer cocaine over no cocaine. Lastly, rats will continue to consume cocaine until it kills them. Therefore, we can determine cocaine would have the same effect on mankind. Time to start a war on drugs? Not exactly.

You see, the flaw with the whole study is it didn't take into account how isolation would fuel the addiction to cocaine. Each one of the rats was in individual cages with nothing to do but drink water or take cocaine. What else were the rats supposed to do? Could it be that, when God put His stamp on all of His creation, He intended its inhabitants to be connected to one another the same way He is?

Then the researchers doing the experiment made an important change to their study. They looked at the isolation factor and asked, "What if we created connection; would these rats have the same propensity to addiction?" The answer was shocking. The scientists created a place called "Rat Park." It was basically rat paradise. They had dozens of other rats to play with, wheels to run on, and tubes to scale. Essentially, they created Disneyland for these rats. The researchers again provided one water bottle with cocaine and one with plain water and observed to see if the altered conditions changed the rats' behavior. They discovered, when the rats were allowed to be social and active, they almost never drank from the cocaine water! In fact, throughout the duration of the second experiment, not a single rat died in Rat Park.

Addiction has less to do with the substance and more to do with a lack of connection. Connection is a basic human need and, when we don't have it, we seek out ways to numb the feeling of isolation and sadness. God spells out clearly what happens when we isolate ourselves:

"THE OPPOSITE OF ADDICTION ISN'T SOBRIETY;

it's connection."

Two are better than one, because they have a good reward for their labor. For if they fall, one will lift up his companion. But woe to him who is alone when he falls, for he has no one to help him up. Again, if two lie down together, they will keep warm; But how can one be warm alone? [32]

It doesn't take much to understand that togetherness is better than loneliness. One of the first things God ever said was, "It is not good for man to be alone." We were made for connection!

For most of my life, I believed deep down I wasn't very good at relationships. I would look at other people I knew, and the deep friendships they had, and be envious. I felt like I missed the day in school when everyone got the manual saying how to do connection with others. Like so many other people, we fall into the trap of, *What's wrong with me?* I realized I carried the same fear of truly being known—fear of vulnerability—that my teammate did. *People are scary. It's best to keep everyone at a safe distance. If people really knew who I was, they wouldn't like me . . .* went the thoughts through my mind, on and on and on. And, while isolation was miserable, it was familiar and comfortable. It felt safer to be the rat alone in a cage than be known by unfamiliar rats in an unknown world.

The environment I was in at the time didn't exactly help me form life-giving connections. When I got into the NFL, I had new friends coming out of the woodwork. People I barely knew

---

33   *Proverbs 18:1, NKJV*

would brag to others they knew me. People were asking me for favors left and right as if they were my closest companions! It made it terribly challenging for me to identify whom I could really trust. I had no clue how to manage the sudden position of influence I found myself in.

The locker room wasn't any easier to deal with. My wife would hear me groan as I awoke each morning before going into work, because I dreaded the intensity I was about to experience. In the NFL, you are evaluated on every single decision you make. You are watched constantly. People monitor who you talk to, how you eat, how you interact with the janitor, and whether you took the stairs or the elevator. My life was a 24/7 job interview and, boy, was it debilitating.

INSIDE THE INTENSITY

On the morning of January 18th, 2015, before the NFC Championship game, the locker room buzzed with anticipation. After a slow start to the season, we found ourselves back in the same place as we were the previous season—one game away from the Super Bowl. As much as we told ourselves, *This game is no different from a preseason game,* you couldn't help but notice the intensity in the air. Little did we know, this game would go down as one of the most insane moments in football history.

The start of the game was atrocious. Nothing was going our way. Turnovers on special teams, interceptions, and penalties. This was not the typical Seahawks team we were used to seeing in crunch time. During my tenure with the Seahawks, our team was 14-2 in prime time games. Clearly, we were pretty good at rising to the occasion. But by halftime, we were down 16-0 to the Packers, desperate for something—anything—to go our way.

All season long, we had been practicing a fake on field goal. Each team usually has a "go to" they can pull out at just the right moment. For us, that moment came in the third quarter with a fourth and ten on the Packers' 19-yard line. It was just the spark we needed to create some excitement.

I snapped the ball to our holder, Jon Ryan. As Steve Hauschka swung his leg through, Jon picked up the ball and scrambled out to his left, leaving him one-on-one with AJ Hawk, a Green Bay linebacker. Jon lobbed the ball up into the air to a wide open Gary Gilliam, and the result was the first Seahawks touchdown of the game.

While the play gave us momentum, with four minutes left in the game, the score remained 19-7. But with a little late magic, we were able to get Russell Wilson into the end zone on a one-yard run to make the score 19-14. Whew! Things were moving.

The sideline and stadium were electric. This was the Seahawks team we were all used to seeing! With 2:09 and one timeout remaining in the game, we chose to do an onside kick. Steve's kick was great. As it was about to go directly into the hands of Jordy Nelson, tight end Brandon Bostick jumped up for the ball. The problem was that, during the play, it was his responsibility to block for Nelson and not go for the ball. When he went for the ball, it cost them. The ball ended up bouncing off his helmet and went right into the arms of one of our wide receivers, giving us a first down at mid-field. Insanity ensued.

From there, it took just four plays to score on Marshawn Lynch's 24-yard touchdown run with 1:25 remaining on the clock. We decided to go for two to make sure the Packers couldn't beat us with a last minute field goal. Russell Wilson got flushed out of the pocket and was forced to run backwards and to the right sideline. Just before being hit, he launched a floating pass from the 17-yard line to the opposite side of the field. Our tight end, Luke Willson, caught Russ' pass at the one-yard line and took the ball into the end zone to give us a 22–19 lead.

After the kickoff, the Packers' Aaron Rodgers completed two 15-yard passes to Randall Cobb and Jordy Nelson. Then Rodgers scrambled 12 yards to our 36-yard line. Following two incompletions and a six-yard throw to Nelson, Mason Crosby kicked his fifth field goal of the day, tying the score at 22–22 with 14 seconds left on the clock and sending the game into overtime.

As we went out for the coin toss, everyone on the sideline, the athletic trainers included, was losing it. The excitement was palpable. We ended up winning the coin toss and Russell Wilson connected with Jermaine Kearse on a 35-yard reception for a walk-off touchdown. An earthquake of elation filled the entire city of Seattle.

Sounds exhilarating, right? And in many ways, it was. But from the moment we arrived at the stadium for the NFC Championship until the following day, I don't think my pulse dropped below 180 beats per minute. My dad told me he will never forget how snippy I was after that game. He was shocked that I didn't seem excited to go back to the Super Bowl. Honestly, I probably was a jerk. I don't remember much from the end of the game till we left for Super Bowl 49 the following week. While part of me was excited to go back, the part my dad saw was the part of me that was absolutely terrified for the amount of stress and pressure I knew I was about to face.

GOIN' TO ARIZONA WITH

AN ACHIN' IN MY HEART[34]

As I mentioned earlier, a Super Bowl itself is stressful enough. Super Bowl 49 felt like stress on steroids.

Flying back home with the Seahawks the day after our stunning loss to the Patriots was an absolute blur. As I slouched lifelessly in my seat, I turned on the movie *Fury*, a movie about a tank operator during WWII, starring Brad Pitt. I couldn't help but understand what these men—the tank operators—went

------

34   *Borrowed from the Led Zeppelin song "Going to California"*

through. The stress those guys were under was on a whole different level. Make a mistake there, and you get blown up.

What I found fascinating was how the men in the movie chose to deal with their stress. Some turned to booze, some to religion, some to women, you name it. They did whatever they could do to take their minds off the fact that their days were numbered. They would say back and forth to each other, "This is the best job I ever had," as if repeating the lie often enough would solidify it as truth. It sounded eerily familiar to me.

Of course, to compare the stress we went through as NFL players to what those guys went through in WWII is offensive. What those men went through was inhuman, and they are American heroes. However, on a biological level, you could argue the stress was similar. I mentioned earlier about guys on the team having "nervous bowl movements"? When you have that in response to stress, it means your brain thinks you are being chased by a bear, and are about to die. I couldn't help but see parallels between my world and theirs.

About midway through the movie, I realized I needed help. The team sports psychologist would say, "Just focus on your breath, trust the process, fake it till you become it," and every other self help mantra under the sun. Why weren't those things working for me, though? Why couldn't I find relief from my torment?

It seemed like no matter how hard I prayed, nothing changed. I guess, in a way, I was just like one of those isolated rats in the science experiment; I went from idol to idol, looking for comfort and never really finding true rest. I couldn't figure out why I wasn't maintaining any momentum. I continually found myself depressed, stressed out, bound-up, and alone.

DEALING WITH IT

I'm thankful for the work and ministry of a place called Onsite where I had the privilege of spending six days after my revelation while watching *Fury* on the flight back from the loss to the Patriots.

Onsite is sort of a mix between summer camp for adults and a deep tissue massage for your soul. I had heard about it from lots of people, but didn't quite know what to expect for my own experience. When I arrived, I cautiously walked through the door to a big room full of unfamiliar people. Thoughts of judgment and fear raced through my mind. *I wonder what they're here for? She looks like a mess. I'm sure my issues are so small compared to that guy's. . .*

Isn't it funny what fear does to us? Fear may be familiar, but it isn't your friend. It may motivate you temporarily, but it will rob you of everything you hold dear. It causes us to forget that deep down, everyone is dealing with the same things: *Do I have what it takes? Am I enough? Does my life matter?* These are questions everyone seems to feel.

At Onsite, the facilitators had everyone get into groups of nine in individual rooms. What they've found with healing trauma is: if you want to get something healed, you actually need to re-experience those painful moments to re-program how your brain sees them. We did this awkward exercise called a "sculpt" where you act out a scene from your life with some-one there to guide and interject truth when it's needed. It feels just as weird as it sounds, but everyone feels uncomfortable with it so at least you're in it together.

I was probably the fourth person to go in the exercise. It was unbelievable how quickly people were brought to tears at each of their healing processes. Each time, the therapist was giving assurances of the great work they were doing, smiling and nodding and encouraging more courage to open up to the monster that had kept so many bound in deep sadness.

When I began to act out my scene, I found myself launched into grief I didn't even know I could experience. Arrested by pain, I couldn't say a complete sentence without crying in front of eight complete strangers. I broke with a deep cry that took my breath away. I glanced up at the therapist who wiped tears from her eyes as she watched me squirm under the weight of pain I couldn't hold any longer.

Admittedly, my competitive side patted me on the back for getting the therapist to cry over my "sculpt" (classic guy, always trying to win at something). However, that little win

"Your

vulnerability

can be the

catalyst

to another's

freedom and

your own."

#BECOMINGBOOK

wasn't enough distraction from how terribly painful, yet cathartic, it was. The anxiety leading up to the moment of opening up my world to total strangers had created such a sense of dread, like when a doctor moves your arm around to confirm it's broken. It hurts like crazy, but it must be done. In a similar way, vulnerability is terrifying. But like anything else, when our greatest fears come true, they're never really as bad as we think they'll be.

The pain I processed at Onsite was the same kind of pain I had witnessed many of my teammates carry, too. Sadly, on one of the biggest stages in the world, many hide their pain behind their accomplishments, routines, and processes. But what is an accomplishment if, deep down, it's just a cover for your pain? Is it really success at all? If you win a Super Bowl but are consumed with depression, isolation, and addiction, what's the point?

Everyone carries a degree of brokenness with them—products of the actions of others and/or our own bent towards managing fear in destructive ways. The good news is we can all be put back together again. "Becoming" whole starts with authentic, meaningful connections with others. But how can you have connection if you don't allow yourself to be fully known? Unless you courageously admit you need someone else's strength, you will forever be isolated, a slave to your own diminishing willpower. And just like a rat in a cage, it can result in decay, addiction, and more.

BEING REAL WITH OUR DOUBTS AND SCARS

After Jesus was resurrected, He visited many people, proving He was God by fulfilling ancient prophecy that after three days the Messiah would rise from the grave. But not everyone was quick to believe. In fact, one of the most notorious doubters was one of His own disciples!

To be honest, I feel badly for Thomas. He gets a bad rap in my opinion. A lot of people refer to him as "Doubting Thomas," which I think is completely unfair. This poor guy is going to live through all eternity with people coming up to him saying, "Hey! You're Doubting Thomas!" I wonder if Thomas is still thinking, *Jeez, I make one mistake and now I'll never live it down!*

When doubting Tommy heard about the miracle, his response was, "Unless I see the nail holes in his hands, put my finger in the holes, and stick my hand in His side, I won't believe it."[35] He didn't believe God was going to do what He said, even though he spent years with God in the flesh.

I actually respect Thomas for being real with his doubts. He was incredibly honest with himself and his struggles with his closest community. Although he was wrong in what he said, he was right in bringing it out into the open with people he trusted. When Jesus finally showed up to him personally eight

---

35   *John 20:25, The Message*

days later, Thomas was blown away and voiced his deep conviction that Jesus was, in fact, the Savior.

If Thomas, who physically walked with God, struggled with doubt, I think you can give yourself a break when you struggle with it. Jesus doesn't shame you for doubting Him. He is totally secure in who He is and can handle your doubt. God is the one who carries you in this relationship, not the other way around. He will show up in your life smiling and saying, "I told you I'd never fail you!"

It took Jesus showing Thomas His scars for Thomas to believe Jesus was who He said He was. Had Thomas not seen the proof of the pain Jesus had gone through, he would have continued to have a hard heart. My question to you is this: What is the "proof of pain" you have in your heart that you are too afraid to open up about? With whom do you need to share your doubts? And to whom do you need to reveal your scars?

As long as you resist vulnerability, pretending to be someone you are not, you will never become the person you have been destined to be. There are people in your life who will not be set free unless you show them your scars. By opening up your wounds, you create hope and connection (the fuel for freedom), not only for others but also yourself.

Don't believe the lie that if people really knew who you are they wouldn't love you. In fact, the opposite is true. Believe it, cling to this truth, and begin to uncover what lies deep within you. Connect with others and invite them to join you on this journey to freedom.

As I have opened up and showed you some of my own "scars," it's my most sincere hope that you will be inspired to open up about your own pain with someone you trust. Some will scoff at this chapter, but the majority of you will experience connection and hope. You are the ones who make it worth the risk of being misunderstood.

Authentic intimacy, real relationship, and true freedom cannot happen without vulnerability. By opening up your wounds, you create hope and connection—the fuel for healing. Your vulnerability can be the catalyst to another's freedom and your own.

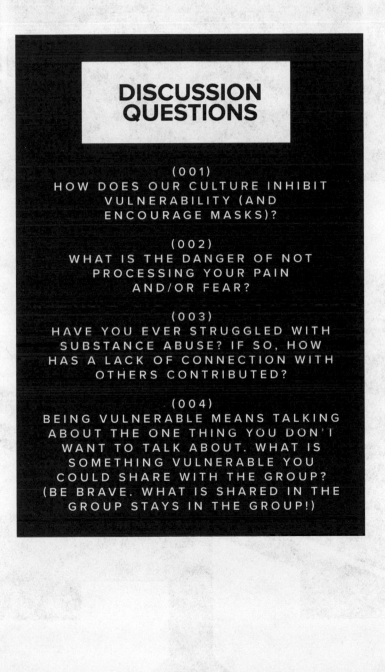

DISCUSSION QUESTIONS

(001)
HOW DOES OUR CULTURE INHIBIT
VULNERABILITY (AND
ENCOURAGE MASKS)?

(002)
WHAT IS THE DANGER OF NOT
PROCESSING YOUR PAIN
AND/OR FEAR?

(003)
HAVE YOU EVER STRUGGLED WITH
SUBSTANCE ABUSE? IF SO, HOW
HAS A LACK OF CONNECTION WITH
OTHERS CONTRIBUTED?

(004)
BEING VULNERABLE MEANS TALKING
ABOUT THE ONE THING YOU DON'T
WANT TO TALK ABOUT. WHAT IS
SOMETHING VULNERABLE YOU
COULD SHARE WITH THE GROUP?
(BE BRAVE. WHAT IS SHARED IN THE
GROUP STAYS IN THE GROUP!)

BETTER TOGETHER

In the story of creation, the Bible tells us over and over, "And God saw that it was good." God created and then sat back and announced He was pleased with what He had created. Then came the crowning achievement in all of His creation: mankind. That's when God said, "Let us make human beings in our image, to be like us."[36]

It's interesting that He said, "Our image," and not, "My image." God wasn't alone in Heaven when He decided to create. God didn't make humans because He was lonely and needed something or someone to stroke His cosmic ego with worship. He created us because He wanted to love us and wanted to see His image represented on the earth.

But when He breathed life into Adam, God looked at this particular part of creation and said, "It's not good." Something was missing. Man was in a deficit. Man needed what God had—community. God knew if His creation was going to thrive, Adam was going to need someone who could stand face to face with him and co-habit the garden God made for them.

---

36   *Genesis 1:26, NLT*

I would even argue that we weren't "fully" created in God's image until God made woman. Ladies, WE NEED YOU.

So the Father, Son, and Holy Spirit looked at each other and said, "It's not good for man to be alone; we will make him a helper to complete him." After that, God went on to create woman. So then the only part of God's creation made in His image was truly a representation of Himself. Man had community. When God said it wasn't good for man to be alone, He was indicating that a good thing can be a bad thing when it's isolated.

The dangers of isolation are many, as I mentioned in chapter 8 in relation to vulnerability. Ecclesiastes 4:12 says, "Though one may be overpowered by another, two can withstand him. And a threefold cord is not quickly broken" (NKJV). We need other people, and isolation is the first step towards the demise of any person of impact.

Community, on the other hand, is the furnace of our sanctification. ("Sanctification" is just a fancy Bible word for becoming more like Jesus.) It's easy to not get offended with people if you never let people get close to you. It's easy to exhibit the fruit of the Spirit when there is no one around to challenge your patience. Without community, we have no one to sharpen us and reflect back to us who we really are.

When I was in seventh grade and playing football at Hamlin Middle School, we won the city championship. I was the quarterback, but we really won because we had a few players who were absolute studs on defense and running back. For a long time, I wondered what had happened to those guys. Then a few years ago, I ran into my eighth grade football coach, who told me he'd seen a car chase on TV and it turned out the guy they were chasing was one of our seventh grade team's running backs! Sadly, he had gotten involved in gangs.

Why do people do that? Why do they blow incredible potential with stupid decisions like joining gangs? It's generally from the very real hunger for connection; unfortunately, gang life is a connection based on hate rather than love.

Isolation decays life more than any drug or drink. Isolation is birthed from continual fear of man in our lives that says: *People are not safe.* Isolation whispers lies that no one else is going through what I'm going through. But the reality is that, behind everyone's perfectly manicured social media, they are facing the same or similar problems you are facing.

LIGHT HEALS

For many, our most pressing need can be the thing we fear the most. That was certainly true for me when it came to community.

My first year with the Seahawks created a chasm in me with regard to people. I already found it difficult to trust people, but, when you add to it the notoriety that comes with pro athletics, well-intentioned people can turn into consumers. I've known many team members who feel the same way—unsure if they can trust, so they stay alone and "safe." This is why famous people date other famous people. The truth is everyone is a local somewhere. The most famous person in the world is not famous to that person's mom. It's just her son or daughter. The key is to treat people with influence just like you would treat anyone else. It helps bridge the gap.

During my rookie year, I really didn't know what was happening inside me. I knew I needed people but, at the same time, was scared to connect. I knew about a young adult service happening on the University of Washington campus. When I pulled up to the campus, I sat in my car because I was afraid of going into the service and possibly meeting new people. I missed the whole service and decided to drive home, feeling worse than I did when I left for church in the first place. Fear will make you do ridiculous things.

Years ago, I met one of my heroes, and we had a chance to sit down and get to know one another. One of the questions he asked me was, "Who are your best friends—the ones you do life with?" At the time, I was living alone in a studio apartment. I was miserable there! I would come home after training and feel so alone. I wanted something different but just didn't know how to make it happen. A lot of my life, I'd had this sense that I had to have it all together. Maybe it was learned in church, from performance culture in sports, or just while growing up, but I had a deep sense of needing to "look the part."

My hero could tell I was frazzled, grasping for the "right an-swer." I don't even remember what I said, but I'm sure it was a lie because, at the time, I was really isolated. I walked away from the meeting feeling ashamed at how alone I was and having no clue how to remedy the situation.

That summer, out of the blue, a guy I knew reached out and invited me to move into his house with a couple other guys. They were serving in an organization called Young Life. I didn't know much about the organization; I was just glad to have someone to talk to at night. I had no idea how much that mo-ment would shape the rest of my life. I was suddenly grabbed off the shore and thrown into a deep flowing current full of everything community was designed to do. It was insanely fun and incredibly challenging at the same time. It molded me, and gave me the courage I needed because I was able to see first hand the beauty of uniting your life to other people. While I had teammates going to Vegas and spending hundreds of thousands of dollars on "fun," I was going to high school foot-ball games as a volunteer Young Life leader with people who knew me and cared about me. Proverbs nails it when it says, "A bowl of vegetables with someone you love is better than steak with someone you hate." [37] My teammates in Vegas and I were after the same thing, but only one of us would find last-ing satisfaction. I found the life I was looking for when I took the risk to enter into community.

---

37   *Proverbs 15:17, NLT*

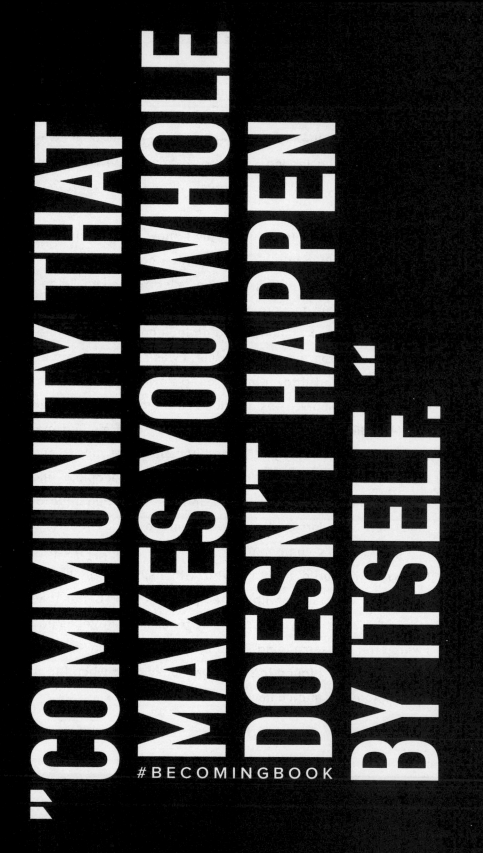

"COMMUNITY THAT MAKES YOU WHOLE DOESN'T HAPPEN BY ITSELF."

#BECOMINGBOOK

ALONE IN A CROWD

One night, I was playing Farkle with the other Young Life leaders I lived with. It was a few years after I moved in with the guys, so the relationships we had were deep. (I ended up buying a house to solidify the presence of Young Life in the community where we were living. To this day, if you drive by the house in Mercer Island, Washington, you will still see the Young Life logo on the dormer with about seven guys sold out for God on the inside.)

Farkle is a dice game that is incredible at breaking down walls with people. but much of that benefit results from the hilarious consequences to the loser. The last person to score enough points has to do an often embarrassing challenge. This particular night, the loser had to take a white shirt, cut out two holes where his nipples were, and walk into a pharmacy to ask the pharmacist where he could find cream for a made-up disease we called "irritable nipple syndrome." The loser had to try and direct the eyes of the pharmacist to his exposed nipples. The rest of us (hiding in the store) struggled to contain our laughter. I don't think I've laughed harder in my life than while seeing an elderly woman blush as my buddy's nipples locked eyes with her.

After our raucous night of fun, I lay in bed and a surprising feeling of sadness came over me. Where was this coming

---

38   *Proverbs 17:22, NKJV*

from? I had just had so much fun. I'd laughed so hard! Even the Bible says laughter is like medicine to our soul.[38] I realized we'd had lots of fun together, but it was totally surface. No one was sharing their struggles and really exposing their hearts to one another. That particular day what I really needed wasn't just fun; I needed connection.

Don't buy the lie that just because you are around other people you are doing life with them. Community that makes you whole doesn't happen by itself. It's a constant fight to stay vulnerable, unoffended, and humble. Real community, capable of launching you into destiny, is going to feel like letting someone hold a .357 to your temple and hoping they don't pull the trigger.

That Young Life house I lived in was wonderful. I realized quickly, though, it wasn't perfect. Even though I was in a crowd, unless I dared to be vulnerable, nothing would change in me. We would have game nights, play Farkle with insanely hilarious consequences, or hang out with kids we were mentoring. But I found sometimes that, even though I was around a lot of people, I still felt alone. I'm sure all of us have felt like that.

If you are an extrovert, this can be a huge obstacle for connection. The false sense of community we get when we are in a busy room is just enough of a counterfeit to keep us isolated. Community means opening up your heart to let people see the worst parts of you. It's incredibly messy but incredibly powerful.

---

39   *Proverbs 27:6, NKJV*

STAY IN THE RIVER

The Bible says, "Faithful are the wounds of a friend; but the kisses of an enemy are deceitful."[39] The truth of that verse seems so counterintuitive. I'll Greshamize it for you: friends will tell you what you need, but don't want to hear; enemies will tell you what you want to hear, but don't need. It's a painful paradox.

Your ability to receive painful truth from friends will determine how far you go in life. The temptation, when you get into "real" community, is to get offended the second it starts to get messy. You decide it's better to be alone than expose your heart to that sort of pain, not realizing that short-term pain will create the long-term strength we are all after in our life.

When David heard the Philistine army was tormenting God's people, even as a young man, he knew it wasn't supposed to be that way. God was in covenant with Israel, which meant He had promised to protect them. All Israel had to do was show up for battle and God would take care of the rest. However, because of the stature of Goliath, the Israeli army was crippled with fear.

When David found out about the rewards for the man who killed Goliath, he was up for the challenge. The story goes that David went out and gathered five smooth stones (apparently choosing five stones because Goliath had four sons) from the brook and went out to confront the one who had been tormenting Israel. With a fire in his belly, David ran towards his enemy and slung the stone, causing the forehead of Goliath to crater from the force of the rock. The precision David displayed in hitting his target was incredible. For him to be just slightly off in his throw might have caused the battle with Goliath to go down differently.

When David approached the brook to gather his stones, the Bible says he chose "smooth stones."[40] The reason he chose the smooth ones in the middle of the brook, as opposed to ones whose edges had not been taken off on the shore, was because he knew he could trust those stones to fly straight and true and accomplish his objective. There were thousands of stones along the banks of the river the current had pushed out to the shore, but those were stones that had not been worn over time in the churning water, causing their hard edges to be smoothed over.

In 1 Peter 2:5, God refers to us as "living stones." In other words, when God chooses servants to accomplish an objective, He goes to the middle of the brook where the smooth stones are, as opposed to the outer banks where the untried, unworked stones with edges are. God selects people who allow the temporary pains of life to work them over and smooth out rough edges. He knows that only "smooth stones" will stay true to their course. If we allow ourselves to drift to the outer banks, isolating ourselves out of pride or fear of being known

---

40   *Samuel 17:40, NKJV*

by others or being offended, God will call others to fulfill His purposes instead of us.

We must sit in the deep flow of community and not retreat to the counterfeit safety on shore if we want to experience all life has for us. It means having the courage to go out and meet someone new or choosing to work through conflict. It means not cutting people out of your life when they fail to meet your expectations. It means realizing life is best lived when you live it with others.

Our brain is constantly trying to protect us. When we do something courageous and we end up getting hurt, our brain will do everything in its power to keep us from repeating the activity. Like the child who touches the hot stove, it can be tough to open up again when we open up to community and get hurt. When we find ourselves retreating to the shores after offense and pain, the mature part of our souls must have compassion for the pain and lead us back to the community we crave. It is only in community where we will see our deepest pains healed and experience our highest joys.

My buddy Rocky, who coached for the Seahawks, used to do meetings for the team where he would show animal clips from the Internet and then put football fundamentals to them. It was a funny way of teaching on a subconscious level. He would show a video of an eagle grabbing a fish and say how we must have great "grip strength" or a clip of a bull about to charge something and yell, "Low man wins!"

A team favorite, though, was when he would play videos of leopards or lions chasing a herd of gazelles. Everyone on the team wanted to see that gazelle get thrashed. In hot pursuit, the prey would, for no apparent reason, suddenly break away from the herd. That gazelle was about to get it. The big cat would catch up to the gazelle and Rocky would shout, "Attack the hip!" As the cat swatted its giant paw at the back hip of the gazelle, we were reminded to attack the hip of a player we were tackling.

I always noticed a deeper truth to the demonstrations, though. It was always the lone gazelle that got eaten! You would never see the lion eat the whole group; it was always the one that broke away and went off on its own.

I see this all the time with people I mentor. Kids show up excited about growing for a little while. Eventually, I quit hearing back from them. Unfortunately, it's when they experience some shame that they feel compelled to stop connecting with people. I learned that one kid I quit hearing from was drowning in addictions. My heart broke when I heard that. He drifted too close to the shore. His rough edges never were smoothed because he chose to isolate himself and withdraw from community with people who were helping him become whole.

JUMP IN! NOTHING EXCITING HAPPENS ON SHORE

There is a town a few hours outside of Seattle called Leavenworth, a Bavarian city that is the place to be during the

Christmas season. There are also a lot of great rivers around there. One summer, I decided to take Matti to Leavenworth for a rafting trip.

We got up early for the endeavor and, when we arrived, climbed eagerly aboard the raft. The water was frigid from the snowmelt. As we journeyed down the river, I started to get a bit bored because Matti and I were both craving a hit of adrenaline. It was an entire 30 minutes of floating before we hit the first rapid. It lasted about 25 seconds but those 25 seconds were an absolute party.

We ended up hitting seven sets of Class Three rapids. Not insane, but still a blast. However, the total time of actually going through rapids was probably five minutes, while the remaining few hours we just drifted. It wasn't that the time of drifting was bad; it was just that being in the rapids was way more fun.

That's how it is in life, as well. It can be tough for many of us to step back into the flow of community. But when we hit those "mainstream rapids" in the company of others, it's thrilling!

Becomers are ones who have chosen to do what's healthy and rewarding in spite of how scary it is. But the more you decide to choose what is courageous over what is safe, the easier it will be.

The best way to make this happen is by starting small. No one ever benches 315 their first try. You have to lift the bar before you get to that. If you want to stand in the face of the "giants" that are keeping you isolated, it means doing one small courageous act every day.

Apply this principle to anything, but make sure you apply it to community. Bravely venture out into the depths of real connection with people. It's way more fun in the rapids than it is on the shore.

DISCUSSION QUESTIONS

(001)
WHAT HAS BEEN YOUR EXPERIENCE
WITH CREATING AUTHENTIC
CONNECTION WITH OTHERS?

(002)
WHO ARE YOUR BEST FRIENDS NOW,
THE ONES YOU "DO LIFE" WITH?
IS THERE A STRONG SENSE OF
COMMUNITY THERE?

(003)
PROVERBS 17:22 SAYS,
"A CHEERFUL HEART IS GOOD
MEDICINE." HOW DOES THIS RELATE
TO LIVING IN COMMUNITY? WHAT
DOES LACK OF COMMUNITY
LEAD TO?

(004)
WHAT IS A SIMPLE NEXT STEP
YOU CAN TAKE TODAY, TO FOSTER
DEEPER CONNECTION WITH PEOPLE
YOU CARE ABOUT?

["I LEARNED THAT COURAGE WAS NOT THE ABSENCE
OF FEAR, BUT THE TRIUMPH OVER IT.
THE BRAVE MAN IS NOT HE WHO DOES NOT FEEL
AFRAID, BUT HE WHO CONQUERS THAT FEAR."]
- NELSON MANDELA

THE CHOICE

New Year's resolutions are so interesting to me. People think, *I'm finally going to lose the weight, be nicer, give more, serve more, read more, and be perfect like everyone else seems to be.* Our culture does such a wonderful job of convincing us that everyone else is doing far better than we are, and we'd better keep up. We compare the entirety of our life to everyone else's social media highlight reel, painfully aware of each one of those tender fail points.

On average, we have between 50,000 and 80,000 thoughts a day with 80% of those being negative. Sometimes negative thoughts are our brain's way of protecting us from danger and keeping us alive. But, while the defense mechanism for identifying threats has helped us stay alive, it hasn't helped us enjoy life. If anything, it has caused all types of insecurities and FOMO (fear of missing out).

I consider myself incredibly lucky that social media wasn't a thing when I was a teenager. I didn't need another channel showing me I wasn't enough, or another false comfort with the illusion of significance for me to build my life upon. Eventually, with enough exposure to everyone else's perfectly constructed social media world, we come to the conclusion we are incapable of changing and "becoming" the person we were destined to be. The frustration can be maddening when we find ourselves still battling the same thing year after year while everyone else seems to have arrived.

GOLIATH ON LINE ONE

On New Year's Eve of 2016, I lay in bed dreaming about how 2017 was going to be different. Planning how I was going to confront all of my fear and make the resolution to do hard things. Like everyone else in America, I was excited at the idea of 2017 being different. This was going to be my year.

Over the course of the 2016 football season, I would vacillate between wanting to watch Seahawks games and being depressed over the very mention of the word "Seahawk." I couldn't believe how high and low I could get after being cut by the team. There was never a doubt in my mind of my ability to throw a football between my legs. But intense emotional events are healed by time, and, by this point, I felt whole and ready for my next pursuit in football.

Throughout the year, I received hundreds of social media messages before and after just about every game from people saying how much I was missed on the team—that things weren't quite the same without me. Many wondered why I had been released and why I hadn't been brought back, when there seemed to be such a need for it.

On New Year's day, 2017, my courage door was kicked in. It was a Sunday, and that day the Seahawks were playing their final game against the 49ers at Levi Stadium. I looked down at my phone around 8:00 pm to see I had a voicemail from a number in the Seattle area. As I listened to the familiar voice of one of the Seahawk scouts, whom I had known for years, I had a surge of emotions. The Seahawks were placing their long snapper on the injured reserve list and wanted me to play in the wildcard game against the Detroit Lions in six days.

When you hope for something for such a long time, it can be shocking when it actually happens. The team that had cut me wanted me back! My old teammates and coaches needed me again! My opportunity to return to an incredible organization and play in front of the greatest fans in football was here. I couldn't believe it was happening.

But as I dialed the number for the Seahawks scout, I had a heaviness in my heart. When he picked up, there was an urgency in his voice. He told me the story and my heart raced. After he finished talking, I had to tell him, "Man, I don't think I can help you guys. I found out just yesterday I tore my labrum in my snapping shoulder. . . "

You see, three weeks before, on a Wednesday, I had been doing a military press, the same way I had done it every

Wednesday for the four months leading up to that day. As I went to rack the weight, I felt a pop in my shoulder. It hurt. I thought with time it would get better, but it never did. Eventually I got an MRI and, while at the dog park with my pup, Bear, 24 hours before the Seahawks called, my doctor told me I would need surgery.

This was one of the most painful and emotionally charged circumstances I've experienced—having to say no to one of the biggest hopes I'd ever had, hopes of getting back into a world in which I felt I belonged. While I wanted to tell everyone the team wanted me back, I was advised to not reveal I needed surgery because it might dampen other teams' interest in me.

Sadly, I told him how thankful I was to get the call, and how good it was to connect again. It was a raw moment. I was so conflicted. While part of me was sad to pass on the opportunity, another part felt relieved. Then another small part of me felt vindicated that I was just out of reach when the team that had cut me needed me again.

The relieved part of me was thinking, *What if I went back and failed?* People saying how much I was needed would instead be saying, "Wow, what happened to Clint Gresham?" or whatever else they would say in disappointment of my performance. The people who once said they loved me might hate me.

In fact, while I had a legitimate reason to pass on the opportunity (once I had gotten a physical, they would have known

I was injured unless I lied, which I didn't want to do), I also recognized that, deep down, part of me was hiding behind my injury. Just below the surface, I kind of felt like maybe it would be better to just ride off into the sunset and close the chapter in Seattle for good. I had gotten everything I hoped for out of my time with the Seahawks, and maybe this was one of those necessary endings.

I woke up the next morning angry at myself, thoughts swirling through my mind. *I wonder if I could do it? My doctor says I need surgery, though.* I finally found myself having to answer a simple question: *Is fear leading me or is God? Am I sabotaging a God opportunity because I'm afraid I may not measure up?* I had to admit the latter was partially true. The start of 2017 was already providing me a prime chance to decide whether I would choose courage or fear.

The next morning, I reached out to the scout and told him, "Hey bro, I haven't tried snapping, but if you guys want to try and work me out to see if I could help, I would be willing to come up there." He called me later that night and told me they were going to see how the other guy they brought in did. Dang.

The next day, I got up and immediately went to the gym to test out my snapping shoulder. I got warmed up, walked into the empty gymnasium, taped a piece of paper against the wall, and began snapping footballs from half court. I took the video, and sent it to the scout, the GM, the position coach, and a few

YOU ARE LESS ALONE THAN YOU REALIZE.

#BECOMINGBOOK

guys on the team, in an attempt to assure them I could do the job against the Detroit Lions in a few days. My agent, Kevin Gold, one of the best agents in sports, also gave me the go ahead to post it across all my social media platforms, saying, "It couldn't hurt." Maybe with the support of Seahawks fans, something could happen.

Shortly after I posted it across Facebook, Instagram, and Twitter, it had well over 60,000 views. I felt confident it was going to happen. I was ripping that football right on target! I needed surgery, but I could also still sling the ball like I always have.

I felt proud of myself—not for snapping well, but for putting myself out there. I did the opposite of what my fear tried to force me to do. I let the team and the GM know I could do it. I was absolutely ready to go. Even though fear had made me hesitate, I was glad I'd made an attempt towards running at what I was afraid of.

That night, I got a text from the team saying, "We signed the new guy; hope you and Matti are well." I felt crushed.

TODAY . . . WE COURAGE

The entire week after that call from the Seahawks was filled with so much self loathing. *If I were just a little stronger, if I had only jumped immediately at the opportunity, or if I just hadn't been such a coward, I could have had an amazing story to tell people of how wonderful I was. Down the road, they would do a movie about me, and I would help millions of people do the opposite of their own fears as well.* But I didn't do that. I got scared and, just like Adam in the Garden of Eden, I hid from God. That day I was reminded how costly fear really is.

While I know now God works everything out for our good, saying no to the Seahawks was so tough! After I had my surgery, the doctor told me it was much worse than he'd thought and it was a good thing I didn't play in that condition. Hearing those words was a healing balm to my frustrated heart. Even though I hadn't jumped on the opportunity, God used my fear to protect me from a bigger problem.

I think far too many of us have bought into the lie that life is happening to us and not for us. It keeps us in this perpetual state of victimhood and self pity that can be so tough to rise above. Because we choose to believe we are the tail being wagged by the dog, we fail to recognize our choice. We have been given a life and given free will to choose what we want life to look like.

For many, decisions were always made for us and we were never given a voice. I think this is especially true of many millennials, who can for this reason feel terrified of "adulting." This lack of experience in "being" is the reason that presenting our adult self (the one who has an opinion and believes it can courage at will) can prove intimidating to some. But when something scary comes along, we do not have to stay stuck in fear. We have the free will choice to decide whether or not we are going to be courageous.

Our greatest fears are usually based in a distorted reality. For example, we think, *If someone really knew who I was, they wouldn't love me.* But we find out that our biggest moral failings are experienced by millions of people every day battling the same exact things. We are all members of the same flawed, universal family, and you are less alone than you realize. What is required of us is to accept the fact that courage is a choice. And life has this beautiful way of presenting doors of opportunity to practice courage, which we can choose to walk through or not.

Hesitation will crush you if you let it. I didn't have it settled in my heart what I wanted, and, because of that, I hid when an opportunity presented itself. One of the greatest challenges we face is being aware of courage opportunities when they show up and having it settled in our hearts to do the brave thing long before the chance arrives. Windows of opportunity are exactly that: a window that opens and closes.

More than anything, I think the opportunity isn't what's on the other side of the window, but the window itself. The *real* opportunity is choosing courage over comfort. It isn't about the specifics of the situation; it's about whether or not you decided to be brave when that window opened.

I don't have the rest of this story for you yet. While I may never have a chance to play professional football again, what I will have is another shot at something scary. Realizing that has absolutely delivered me from regret. God used the Seahawks as a tool, not as a prize. It's choosing courage that delivers the prize—self respect. I thank God that more chances for that are always coming my way and yours.

How do you feel with your current situation? Would you rather stay inside where it's warm and familiar, or jump through a window where you might fall? No one ever raved about a movie where the protagonist sat around refusing to confront anything scary. Everyone hates that character. Nobody is winning a Pulitzer Prize without a story of courage. The presence of bravery in our life will be the measure of how full our hearts can be. If we want to be whole in every area of our lives, courage is the beginning.

WE'VE ALL DONE IT

Jonathan was out with his assistant one day and looked up on the top of a great hill and saw a massive number of Philistines, the archenemy of Israel. At that time, Israel was living under God's judgment, including significant persecution from the prolonged Philistine occupancy.[41] Nevertheless, even while reproving their unfaithfulness, God showed Himself strong and faithful to Israel in specific ways.

---

41   *See Judges 2:20-3:3*

While standing there, Jonathan looked at his assistant and said, "Okay, if they call us up there, we will know God is going to help the two us fight and defeat the entire garrison, but if they say they are going to come down to us, we will know it's time to run." (Thinking two people could defeat an entire garrison of trained soldiers is a *bad* military strategy.)

I imagine Jonathan and his assistant grinned at each other as the Philistine officer signaled for them to climb up the mountain for "a little chat." Moments later, Jonathan and his assistant took out a huge number of Philistines and the rest of them retreated over the chaos the two young Israelites caused.

God proved strong and faithful to Jonathan's faith and did the miraculous. However, the only reason He did it was because two guys settled it in their hearts to respond courageously if God called! Had those two guys not taken the first step towards courage, God wouldn't have done anything. What transpired afterwards was that the Israelites, who had been in hiding from the terror of the Philistines, came out of hiding and entered into the fight. One man, throwing up a courageous "Hail Mary," caused an entire nation to face its tormentors by faith.

Days after I got the text telling me the Seahawks were going with a different guy, I thought about this story. For a short time, I felt shame and thought God was probably annoyed with me for playing it safe. But lingering shame and guilt don't build faith and courage. It's times like that we need to under-stand that God takes the longgggg-term approach to our time on Earth.

My whole life, I have been frustrated with my strength training. I've never quite gained the level of strength I wanted or that I thought was expected of me. I knew where I wanted to be but, for some reason, I couldn't close the gap.

After being released from the Seahawks, I found myself in charge of my own workouts, which was the most incredible thing in the world. I was no longer having every move cri-tiqued and could train the way I wanted. My problem under that critical pressure had always been that, when I attempted and failed to step up to a heavier weight lift, I would become discouraged from trying again.

But now that I was on my own, I was patient enough to consid-er taking smaller steps. I would go up about five to ten pounds a week. After months of this, I had gone up at least 60 pounds on all of my lifts. It made me love training again because I was finally seeing the payoff of taking the long-term approach in-stead of forcing the fear-driven quick fix to where I thought I should be.

Courage is the same way. It's a muscle that needs to be exer-cised and slowly increased over a long period of time. When you familiarize your courage muscle to slow, progressive overload, you will begin to see your fears are usually unfounded. The hard things become progressively easier to do. Doing really hard stuff comes from consistently lifting the weight of smaller, less challenging things like having a tough conversation with someone you care about, asking a girl on a date, or even stating an opinion others might think is stupid.

Our courage muscle is built on days and years of consistently exercising a choice to run at the giants in our lives including our own negative self talk. I always loved how, in the story of David and Goliath (the epitome of confronting something scary), the Bible says, "David ran at Goliath." He wasn't hiding behind anything. He knew who he was. He knew what was on the line. He knew he could boldly run at the very thing that terrified all of God's people with the full assurance he could crush scary things. I want to be like that.

Becomers recognize that God knew what He was getting into when He chose to create us, redeem us, and pursue us. They know He takes a long-term approach with us. He is patient. And He doesn't condemn us when we don't stick to the ridiculous standards we hold ourselves to.

Becomers can also take a step back and realize courage is a choice. While there will be disappointment when we get too scared to choose courage, we can trust that life will present other opportunities to step out in faith—opportunities to trust there is a good Father in Heaven who likes us, loves us, and wants to work all things for our good.

When I find myself acting like a giant toddler, throwing a tantrum when God doesn't open the door I want, I can remember that the good times in life are God loving me and the tough times in life are God growing me. I need them both. God opens doors people can't open and closes doors people can't close.

Together, let's settle it in our hearts to lean on God's strength and community, and let's choose to walk in courage. You may fail. I take that back: you will fail. But the pain of initial disappointment will be overshadowed with the surge in self esteem for making the faith-filled courageous choice next time. It will cause strength, grit, and courage to grow, all of which are fundamentals to a life worth living.

Lets choose courage today and choose to be fully alive. After all, we are becoming . . . everything God created us to be.

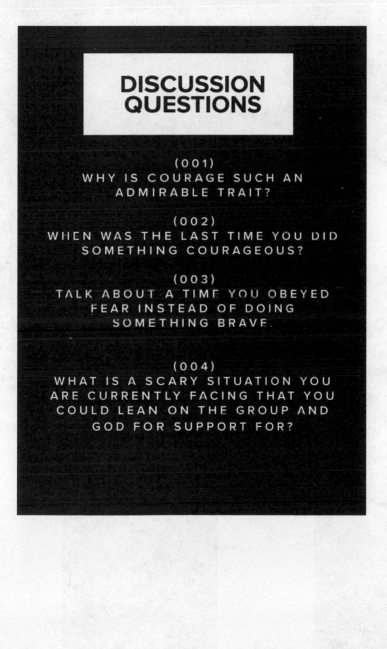

DISCUSSION QUESTIONS

(001)
WHY IS COURAGE SUCH AN
ADMIRABLE TRAIT?

(002)
WHEN WAS THE LAST TIME YOU DID
SOMETHING COURAGEOUS?

(003)
TALK ABOUT A TIME YOU OBEYED
FEAR INSTEAD OF DOING
SOMETHING BRAVE.

(004)
WHAT IS A SCARY SITUATION YOU
ARE CURRENTLY FACING THAT YOU
COULD LEAN ON THE GROUP AND
GOD FOR SUPPORT FOR?

11

CODA

There are moments along the journey of our lives that can make even the strongest of us doubt that God actually cares. Maybe it is the loss of a dream or a loved one, sexual abuse, or a prayer God doesn't seem to answer the way you hoped. It can cause disillusionment in a God who, we are told, wants to make all things new. Like the leper who said to Jesus, "God, I know you can, I just don't know if You want to," we wonder if He even notices our pain.

I think most of us would agree God cares about everyone, generally speaking, but it can be tougher to accept God cares about you as an individual. Sometimes it's easier to have faith for someone else than it is to have faith for yourself. But the truth is that He sees that deep dark part of your soul, the part that carries your deepest pain; He hasn't overlooked or forgotten about it. In fact, when it seems everyone else around you has forgotten it, God looks down with empathy. He is a God that loves to make dead things grow again.

WHEN TRAGEDY STRIKES

Life can be like a beautiful, flower-filled minefield full of beauty as well as danger. One moment you're walking along perfectly happy, then next you find yourself crippled from an unforeseen life blast. When reality hurls blows of defeat and loss, it's a bewildering task to trust a good God who says He is in charge.

For me, that moment came when I was in the second grade. I remember the wind whipping across the rosy cheeks of two seven-year old boys as my friend, Weston, and I raced his family's golf cart across his country property. We felt alive! That particular day, we were hunting seagulls with his dog.

When I say hunt, what I really mean is chase. We got a kick out of scaring those pesky birds. We were in hot pursuit when Weston's dog began to lead them towards the beach. When we lost sight of where the birds were, we decided we'd better hike down to the beach to do some "bird scaring." With our hunting dog leading us, we ran down the hillside onto the beach in our attempt to catch one of the sky rats. Things were going great until, about five steps out onto the beach, the ground below us began to give way, and we started to sink—quickly. Within a matter of moments, we were waist-deep in some type of stinky, quicksand-like mud.

The threat of suffocation by "stink mud" became a very real fear as the scent of rotting fish pummeled our little noses.

Weston sank faster so, with no one around except the laughing seagulls and a preoccupied dog, I knew I had to do something. Weston was depending on me. With my skinny outstretched hand, I grabbed my friend by the shirt and struggled to pull him up. When he was safely on top of the mud, he was able to army crawl back to the base of the hill filled with shrubs and limbs he could grab. My partner in crime reached for the longest branch he could find and then pulled me to shore with him.

As we collapsed on the ridge, completely exhausted and covered in "stink mud," we looked down at our feet and realized the mud had not only stolen our fun but our shoes, too. We looked at each other and laughed while cacophonous sounds of the sky rats mocked us.

The climb back up the hill was arduous. The only friend we had in the moment was our trusty golf cart. It got us quickly back to Weston's country home, where his mother cleaned up two very wet, stinky, shoeless little boys. We were beat in every sense of the word.

Being with Weston was always an adventure. He was my best friend and my little buddy. He was much smaller than I was, and I always felt a duty to protect him. Weston and I did everything together, especially if Ninja Turtles were involved. He was practically a part of our family. My mom threw his mom a baby shower, and his mom did the same for my mom. We were regular kids who did regular kid stuff, in our regular town. But one day, our regular world changed.

I was in the midst of Mario madness (playing Mario Brothers on my Nintendo was an all time favorite for Weston and me) when my mom walked up behind me with tears streaming from her eyes. I was immediately scared. Between gasps for breath, she barely squeaked out, "Clinty, Weston has died."

At first, I didn't understand what that meant. It was my first encounter with the reality of death and the fragility of our being. My mom gripped me tightly and wept. I in turn wept until I had no more tears to give. I felt like a sponge that had been wrung completely dry.

Weston had been on the back of our trusted golf cart, the giver of so much joy, with his little brother. The nanny pushed the gas and, though his brother held on tight, Weston's hands slipped and he fell. As the golf cart rolled away from Weston, he landed on the concrete, slapping the back of his head on the unforgiving surface and knocking him unconscious. He was rushed to the hospital and placed in ICU. When the doctors looked at the scans and saw no activity in his brain waves, they knew Weston was gone.

How do you reconcile the pain of loss with the innocence of childhood? My best friend was gone—gone forever. The very thing that had created so much fun for us was the instrument used to take him away from us all. At Weston's funeral, his younger brother reached up to grab his mom's hand and said, "I was a good boy, Mommy. I held on and didn't go away."

DOWNHILL FROM THERE

Losing Weston was ground zero of a painful chain reaction that ripped through our usually safe and normal world. The day Weston died changed a lot of things. So many things were lost! All the things I felt safe about began to feel like the "stink mud" that had tried to swallow Weston and me whole. Wonder dwindled. Joy was elusive. Safety was fleeting. The world became scary.

Weston's death was also the straw that broke the camel's back in my already fragile family. It shook us to the core. He was such a part of our family that my parents felt they had lost a son, too. A year later, my parents filed for divorce. I remember when they walked into my room and told me. We all cried together.

As I got older, it seemed the pain from Weston's death grew instead of diminished. There continued to be this incessant gnawing of pain that I couldn't get rid of. I tried memorizing Bible verses, talking to counselors, and trying to pray it away. But when your soul gets wounded, the only person who can heal it is the One who made it.

After that came the uphill battle of searching for wholeness. I spent years bound to all types of false comforts, grasping for something to give me a sense of relief. I was looking for a spiritual experience that would connect me to a power greater than myself. I was looking for escape. I was looking for the God of the Bible to reveal Himself to me, to show me He was real, that He saw me, and to communicate that He cared about my pain.

NOT FORGOTTEN

In 2013, I went down to Corpus Christi to speak at a friend's church. I don't make it back home often, so when I do, I always try and hit the spots that are nostalgic for me: the beach, the Surf Club restaurant, and Ray High School. But it had been two decades since I had visited Weston's grave. As a little boy, my mom and I would go by and leave Ninja Turtle action figures at his memorial. He loved those. It always seemed the moments I found myself being introspective, I thought about Weston. I often wondered how life would have turned out had he not died. So while driving through town on this particular trip, I had the urge to visit Weston's grave.

I made my way to Seaside Memorial (the same place the pop singer Selena is buried) in search of a moment to remember and honor my friend. After twenty minutes of trying to remember the location of his gravesite, I began to get weary. There were thousands of sobering conclusions to sort through. I finally decided to ask for help.

In the memorial office, I was greeted by a friendly elderly woman, and I gave her a note with Weston's name and asked for help finding my friend's grave. She smiled and went to find him. After 15 minutes, she came back with an uncertain look in her eyes. She couldn't locate his grave. She went on to say there was no record of a Weston being buried there. I was confused. I knew for certain that was where he was. (When a seven-year-old leaves a prized Ninja Turtle action figure somewhere on purpose, he doesn't forget it.)

Days later, my mom told me that I had actually spelled his name incorrectly. With the correct spelling, I went back to Seaside with a newfound confidence of seeing Weston's grave. I walked into the office of the friendly woman with a smile on my face. She returned the smile and came back with the exact spot he was buried.

As I approached where I thought the map was pointing, I noticed a couple standing over one particular grave, having a moment. They held each other tightly, the man's hand lovingly supporting the woman in his arms. Days before, when I was searching for the grave, I had walked past the exact spot they were standing, as I searched for my friend. I decided to give the couple a wide birth out of respect.

After about 20 minutes of creepily pacing back and forth, a fleeting thought came through my mind. *That would be crazy if those were Weston's parents.* I didn't even remember the last time I saw them. They certainly wouldn't have recognized me after 20 years. As they began to walk away from the grave, I felt a quickening in my heart. They climbed into their SUV and began to pull away. With tail lights fading in the distance, I ran towards the grave they were grieving over. As I stood over the gravesite, my heart melted. The gravestone read "Weston Conoly." After 20 years of not seeing Weston's parents, God had connected us with each other at his grave. I was blown away.

But they were completely oblivious to the God moment that had just happened! I wish my 40-yard dash time at the NFL scouting combine had kicked in at this particular moment. As fast as I could, I sprinted all the way back to my rental car in an attempt to catch up with them. I had another problem, though. *Where on earth did they go?*

The exit leaving Seaside Memorial turns out onto Ocean Drive, which goes the entire stretch of the bay in Corpus Christi. I had two choices: drive towards downtown, or drive out towards Padre Island. One direction would lead me to an encounter with a couple who had been like second parents, the other would lead to a complete waste of time and a deep disappointment. Something within me was reminded of the direction of where Weston's house was. Ignoring all speed limits and stop signs, I took a hard right out onto Ocean Drive towards Padre Island.

While on the familiar road, I prayed a police officer wouldn't happen to drive by as I cruised along at 80 mph trying to catch up to them. Finally, about four miles down the road, I saw their SUV at a stoplight. I pulled up next to them and froze. *What on earth do I do now?!* The light changed and I was overcome with emotion. As we began to drive past the baseball field where Weston and I had played as children, I made a decision.

We were cruising along at about 50 mph and I rolled down my window and honked, waving to try to get their attention. The man driving rolled down the window, completely perplexed with what was going on. As he looked at me, I shouted from my car, "Are you Weston Conoly's parents?" My heart beat like a Travis Barker drum solo as I realized this was probably the first time in decades they had been asked that question. The man driving gazed back at me with pride and sadness at the same time, and promptly responded, "Yes, we are." I shouted back through our open windows, "I'm Clint Gresham."

As soon as I yelled that, Weston's mother leaned forward, screaming shouts of joy and shock. It was one of the most surreal moments of my life. Both of us slowed our vehicles down and quickly drove up onto the curb along the fast moving road. We jumped out of our cars and ran towards each other with tears in our eyes. I hugged Weston's mom and dad for the first time in 20 years. Between chokes for air and divine ecstasy, Weston's mom said, " I feel like I'm hugging my Weston." It was the holiest, most profound moment of my life.

The reason this moment was so powerful for me was that Weston's death had been ground zero for so much of the trauma I had experienced in my life. While I had spent much of my life attempting to deal with symptoms of pain, I had never really gotten to the root of it. Weeds that are cut and not uprooted just reemerge. Wounds that aren't cleansed so as to remove infection may scab over but never totally heal. Twenty years after so much pain, God reached down and healed my wound. I later found out it was the first time Weston's mom had been back to his grave in years. God went back to ground zero, because He doesn't miss a thing. No matter how long it's been, your heavenly Father never forgets about your pain.

CAN YOU EMBRACE YOUR HEALING?

Sadly, deep wounds for some become so familiar they deny themselves healing. In July of 2016, my mom sent me a text message saying to call her immediately. When I called, she sounded frantic. It felt like *deja vu* for some reason. The intensity in her voice reminded me of sitting on my couch playing Mario when she first told me about Weston. As I listened intently, she softly said, "Clint, Weston's mom just took her own life." I was stunned—grieved beyond words at what their family had gone through and what they were going through now. While the moment of seeing Weston's parents again brought healing to my life, it hadn't to hers.

The reality is that, while God is powerful, so is our own free will. I think many of the things we hold God responsible for throughout the world can actually be the consequences of human free will decisions to choose God or not, obey God or not, receive Him or not.

Back in the Garden of Eden, when Adam and Eve made the decision to turn away from Him, decay entered the human experience. Fear didn't exist before that. Shame didn't exist. Agony didn't exist. It was Heaven on Earth. God made Adam and Eve extraordinarily powerful when He gave them free will. Granting them the ability to choose was actually the only way to assure the love they gave would be authentic.

He is presenting each of us with the same decision today. He says to us as He said to His people centuries ago, "I call heaven and earth as witnesses today against you, that I have set before you life and death, blessing and cursing; therefore choose life, that both you and your descendants may live."[42]

When God offers healing, we still have the free will responsibility to receive it. It is our decision and no one else's if we are going to stay in pain, or heal. It doesn't mean the pain automatically goes away. I still cry over Weston, and the pain losing him caused. But I have chosen to allow the pain to push me closer to a God who loves me instead of pushing me deeper into isolation and depression. I love what Pastor Bill Johnson says, "Anything absent of hope is under the influence of a lie." Too many of us have accepted the soothing lie that we are helpless victims and prisoners of our pain when the truth is that we choose to stay in it.

---

42   *Deuteronomy 30:19, NKJV*

We must choose every day the process we will walk in—one that leads to abundant life or one that leads to greater decay.

BECOMING BECOMERS

I have a friend named Mauricio who has overcome remarkable pain and adversity to get where he is. Today, he operates a non-profit called "Tree of Life" on the very plot of land on which his own mother sentenced him to death. There, he offers help and care to single mothers who have no other options.

When Mauricio was born, his teenage mother was alone. She had no one to turn to, no one to trust, and nothing to offer the little boy she was carrying inside her. What was she supposed to do? The father of her baby was an alcoholic serial impregnator who, by the end of his life, had spawned 24 other babies. How could anyone expect her to turn this mistake into a fairy tale ending? She knew nothing of fairy tales. She didn't even have the privilege to dream for a better life. At 15 years old in a small village of Nicaragua, to sell your body to carnivorous men was as close to finding Prince Charming as she would ever get. But her problem would all be over soon.

The day she went into labor, as she stumbled to a tree, the contractions increased in duration and frequency. Pools of sweat dripped down her brow from the heat and humidity of the tropical climate. The thought assault was in full force: God, the devil, friends, and family all hurled their stones at the harlot, seeking to destroy her. She knew it wouldn't be much longer. *It would all be over soon.*

With one final push, the baby inside her breached and hit the ground. Cries reverberated throughout the jungle as if creation itself groaned over the tragedy of what was and what was to come. Asylum was within her grasp. The shrieks pierced her ears but ricocheted off her armored heart. She reached down hastily to her bare feet to pick up the squirming creature that had just come from her body, looking around frantically for somewhere to cleanse herself of her "impurity."

An inkling of selfish hope surfaced as she walked towards what would be the tomb of the crying boy she held in her cold hands. The dilapidated outhouse barely stood on its own as if ashamed of what it was created for. As she opened the door, she felt the cooling anticipation of unburdening herself. She took her new-born baby, Mauricio, and threw him into a pit of human waste. To assure his fate, she took large stones and threw them down into the pit towards her son. Confident she had liberated her-self of all responsibility, she walked away from the outhouse. Her sin was covered. It was all over. Or was it?

The next day, some children who occasionally played near the outhouse came by and heard a baby crying. Shocked to real-ize it was coming from the outhouse, they ran and told their father, who came quickly and climbed down into the hole to rescue the infant. Had it not been for the conscience of that father, an innocent child would have died.

Fast forward many years. Mauricio tells me how he had every right in the world to live as a broken person, replicating his pain in the ways his mother and father did. But Mauricio chose God. He chose to receive God's healing. He decided to put his pain to death and embrace God's love. He chose to embrace the "becoming process" to be the person God had designed him to be. He was no longer chained to his past as a powerless victim.

Mauricio still experiences moments of pain, just as we all do. My point is that what we do with our pain is entirely in our own hands. God will present opportunities through which to nourish and have compassion on us. He is a good God who cares about our felt (day to day) needs and not just about getting us a ticket into Heaven. It's up to us to receive His healing and not tie His hands with our free will decision to stay hurt.

WE CHOOSE

Like Mauricio, "becomers" are ones who have made the decision to choose a tougher right way over an easier way. They choose health over heartache, solace over selfishness, passion over pity, and courage over cowardice. They choose to allow the battered points of their soul to become memorials for a broken world of God's ability to work all things for good.

Let me assure you: hardship will come, but God is never the author of it. He wants to give you a life filled with joy like any dad wants for his kid. Receive it. Embrace it. And remember:

the surest path towards a life of wholeness is found in making the conscious decision to keep "becoming."

> *Dear friends, we are already God's children, but he has not yet shown us what we will be like when Christ appears. But we do know that we will be like him, for we will see him as he really is.*
> *1 John 3:2, NLT*

DISCUSSION QUESTIONS

(001)
WHY IS UNCHECKED PAIN SO DEADLY?

(002)
HOW IS IT TRUE THAT GOD HEALS OUR PAIN, BUT THAT WE HAVE A RESPONSIBILITY TO RECEIVE IT?

(003)
WHY DO WE NEED LOVING ACCOUNTABILITY AND SUPPORT TO HELP HEAL THE PAINFUL WOUNDS WE HAVE EXPERIENCED?

(004)
"BECOMING" THE PERSON WE WERE DESIGNED TO BE INVOLVES A CHOICE OF WHETHER OR NOT WE WILL GROW, OR STAY IN PAIN. WHAT EMOTIONS AND/OR DECISIONS DOES THAT BRING UP FOR YOU?

I've always wondered how the dude with the withered hand must have felt in Mark 3. For this guy's entire life, he existed with something he probably felt *so* ashamed of. His mind consumed with his flaw. Constantly wishing for a particular outcome (a normal hand) to appear so he could finally get some relief from the self hatred he most likely felt.

Ancient Israel wasn't exactly the most emotionally healthy or empathetic society at the time. They were a new country. In many ways, still learning to walk. Self righteous religiousness ruled, while the compassion Jesus taught seemed to be fleeting. I can't say for sure, but it isn't that far fetched to imagine how insecure this man probably felt about his disability.

The thing I love about the word "becoming" is that it's both an adjective and a verb. That word embodies what a beautiful process looks like. Exactly what it means to like yourself in the midst of change, growth, disappointment, and refinement. Being beautiful . . . with character still not perfect, problems still not solved, questions still not answered, and wounds still not healed.

When I talk about loving the process to wholeness, it's easy to assume wholeness is a destination. Everything we have ever been taught has been about outcomes. Cause and effect. Beginning and end. Reap and sow. This and that. What I'm about to say is the lynchpin of emotional success: wholeness has *nothing* to do with a destination.

I'm *so* over trying to finally "arrive" at where culture and my own insecurities demand me to be. It seems most of the peace God has for our fulfillment seems to be connected to how okay we decide to be with things left undone. Wholeness more than anything, is a state of mind, although a difficult one. It means giving up hope for a better past, relinquishing control for a perfect future, and choosing joy and courage right where our feet are. It means setting your heart like a flint to choose joy, courage, strength, and healthy relationships. It means letting God into the dark places, and exposing them to God and friends. The man with the withered hand was never made whole until he showed the one thing he was ashamed of to the only person who could do anything about it. In the same way, this is our mandate. Choosing a life of vulnerability, which is the key to lasting joy.

I pray that this book would be your battle cry in the war against isolation and fear. That it would ignite courage in you to expose your shame for the liar that it is. May we continue to choose God's process in every moment, refusing the path of least resistance to blaze a trail through the thicket of our pain—and in so doing, find the wholeness of soul we crave.

Here's to loving the process.

ACKNOWLEDGMENTS

Matti – my dove. You light up any room with your beautiful and magnetic spirit. I am honored each day at your decision to walk into a life of uncertainty with me. You are so kind and tender to so many people and your love makes me want to be a man. Thank you for encouraging me, sharpening me, and loving me with such grace and understanding. Thank you for modeling godly womanhood and being the greatest gift. I couldn't have done this without your support. I love you forever.

Mom - You did so much to give Brent and me an amazing life. Your sacrifice through so many hard years is one of the most selfless examples of love I have seen. Thank you for being so patient, and for teaching me how to connect with myself and how to be a seeker of truth. You have marked me with what it means to love people. More people need to have your heart.

Dad - I can't think of anyone I have more respect for than you. When I look back on growing up, I see you always put your family before yourself, the true mark of a real man. I want to be like you. Thank you for teaching me hard work and the way of selflessness, and for helping me become a man. If the men of this world were like Jim Gresham, this world would be a wonderful place.

Lisa - Your dedication to the family is astounding. Thank you for stepping into our lives and being a presence of love, for choosing to be an advocate for our family and never giving up even when things got hard.

Phil - I think there is nothing more serendipitous than how you went to Heaven on Father's Day. You were a spiritual father to so many. I remember many late nights needing guidance and you always helped me hear from God for myself. Your willingness to be available has molded me into the kind of influencer I want to be. Thank you. I miss you all the time.

Gregg and Jessica - You both showed me how wonderful walking with God could be. You taught me truths about God, family, and marriage, that will be with me for the rest of my life. Gregg, thank you for being such a consistent voice of encouragement and acceptance. For helping me walk through really dark seasons and doing it with understanding and empathy, just like Jesus. Jessica, thank you for modeling what godliness looks like and for guiding me early on in relationships. For opening up your home to me right after having a kid! You are amazing and your wisdom in just about everything blows my mind. To both of you, thank you for being an example to Matti and me. Gabrielle and Judah, WE LOVE YOU!

The Funks - Todd, Erin, Hayden, Wyatt, Regan in Heaven, and Eli, the month I spent living with your family has marked my life permanently. Your willingness to open up your lives has never left me. You are some of the most generous people I know and I am thankful God brought us into each others' stories. Thank you for being a safe place for me to run to when life around me got hard. For letting me be a part of your family and loving me when I didn't like myself very much. You are some of the finest, strongest, and most loving people I know and a gift to everyone who has the privilege to know you. May God's blessing always shine brightly on you.

Eric - You were like Moses to me, walking me through the wilderness so patiently when I kept going around the same mountain over and over. You never gave up, even when I wanted to. I simply wouldn't have made it to where I am today without you in my life. Your example of simple, consistent, life on life discipleship at Panera Bread, morning after morning, has ingrained in me how to be a strong Kingdom man who rejects passivity, engages with God, accepts responsibility, and leads courageously. Cindy, Taylor, and Madison, you ladies ROCK and Matti and I adore all of you. Thanks for letting us into your world.

Brent - Who you are is absolutely incredible. Your outlook on life, care for others, and passion are an inspiration. I'm so glad we live in the same state again. I'm so proud to call you my brother. I can't wait to walk with you through the rest of our lives together. You're my best pal.

Isabelle - I have loved watching you grow into the strong, compassionate, loving young woman that you are. You are such a fun, wonderful person and I'm thrilled to watch where God takes you in these next few years. Who you are is so wonderful.

Jennings - You are a thousand times bigger on the inside than you are on the outside. Not only do you carry yourself with power, but also with poise. The sky is the limit for you, bro. And I'll be there with you every step of the way.

All the guys in the "Hamquarters" Young Life House - For the men of the past, present, and future, thank you for being willing to be the hands and feet of Jesus to the young people of Mercer Island, Washington. For choosing to give your life away, and see young people get saved before they need to be rescued. For the guys who were there when I was living there, thank you for loving on me and being a wonderful escape from a world that pushed me into such darkness. I needed all of you and thank God for you.

Conolys- To David, Wylder, Will, and Wyatt, thank you for letting me use the story of Weston and Katherine in heaven. They are missed. David, thank you for how you have been a model of how to walk through seasons of pain. My God continue to show His love to you in tangible ways for the rest of your lives.

Marshall and Emily - You came into my life at the perfect time. Thank you for being such a wonderfully safe place for me. For being people I could trust with my mess. For helping me to carry myself with honor and walking with me during just about every disappointment I had over the last few years. Matti and I attribute so much of who we are to your selflessness. May God pour out such a ridiculous level of favor and blessings on your family. We love you.

were a safe harbor. When I found myself bound with things that made me hate myself, you saw me as someone worthy of love. You were a silent supporter who absolutely did not have to do what you did. But you allowed God to use you and it saved my life. I thank God for your kindness, understanding, and empathy. For letting me cry, and walking me through pain. Thank you for cheering me on and for doing it with such grace.

Arlyn - This book could not have happened without you. Thank you for taking everything in me, and laying it all out there, the good and the bad, and helping make sense of so much life. Thank you for being a voice of kindness and gentleness as I walked through the death of my identity in football. Your support, enthusiasm, care, and guidance gave birth to this book which feels like a son to me. I'm forever grateful.

ALSO AVAILABLE:

BECOMING: THE WORKBOOK

This six-session workbook takes *Becoming: Loving the Process to Wholeness* to an interactive level, suitable for mentorship, discipleship, small groups, and personal study. Participants will have opportunities for reflection, journaling, Scripture memory, and practical application of the principles found in *Becoming*, as well as prompts for discussion and prayer.

ITALK CARDS

This 52-card deck of biblically-based affirmations will teach you how to think like God thinks and see your situation as God sees it. In this high performance world, self talk is everything. These practical affirmations will train your self talk to operate out of a renewed mind—and put you on the path to *Becoming* . . . everything God made you to be.

BECOMING WRIST BAND

Spread the word that you are *Becoming* . . . and encourage your friends to become all that God designed them to be, too. Wrist band says "Love the Process" and "I'm Becoming." Sure to spark questions that will give you opportunities to share your journey and speak words of life and hope into others.

To order, visit www.clintgresham.com

Notes

Notes

Notes

Notes

Notes